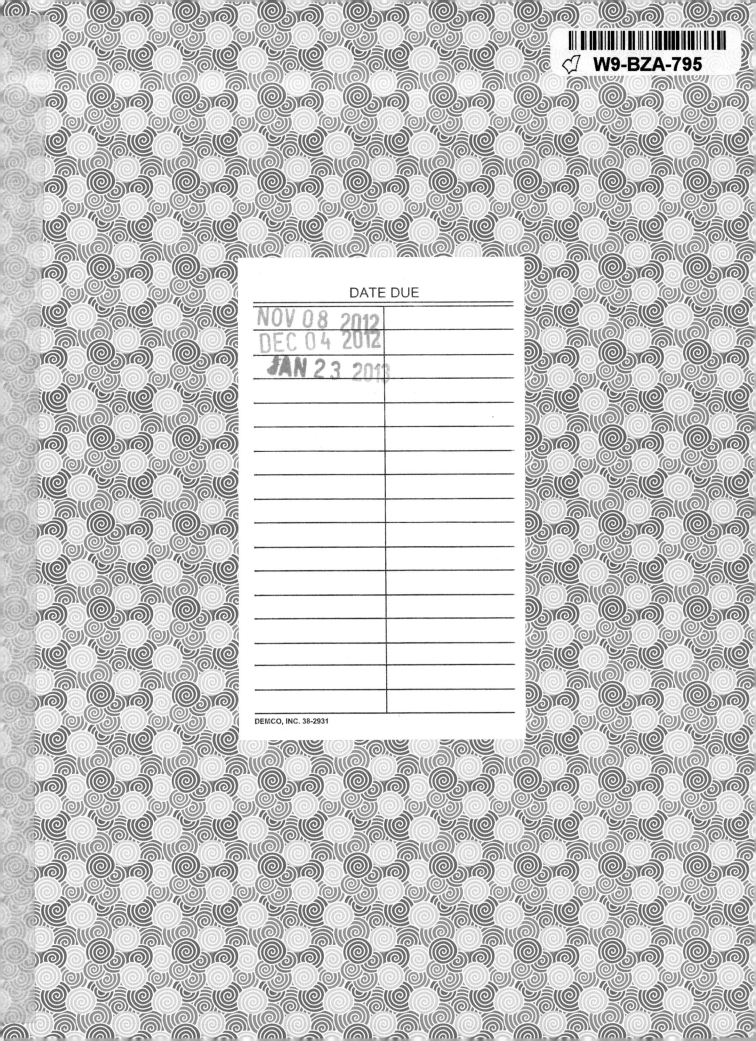

making **vintage** accessories

25 original sewing projects inspired by the **1920s–60s**

making **vintage** accessories

25 original sewing projects inspired by the **1920s–60s**

emma brennan

GUILD OF MASTER CRAFTSMAN PUBLICATIONS

First published 2009 by

Guild of Master Craftsman Publications Ltd

Castle Place, 166 High Street,
Lewes, East Sussex BN7 1XU

Step-by-step photographs by Will Russell
Styled photography by Laurel Guilfoyle

ISBN: 978-1-86108-637-2

A catalogue record for this book is available from the British Library.

Associate Publisher:	Jonathan Bailey
Production Manager:	Jim Bulley
Managing Editor:	Gerrie Purcell
Senior Project Editor:	Virginia Brehaut
Editor:	Naomi Waters
Managing Art Editor:	Gilda Pacitti
Design:	Tonwen Jones

Colour origination by GMC Reprographics
Printed and bound in China by Hing Yip Printing Co. Ltd.

Dedicated to Charlie.
A chip off the old block.

Note:
The patterns in this book are not
meant to be replicas of period
pieces. They are grouped together
in eras simply because they are
influenced by a feature of that
particular period. They are not
necessarily historically accurate
but reflect the mood or look of the
periods they represent.

The author has designed the
original patterns in this book and
owns the copyright to the designs
and pattern pieces. They are for
home and personal use only by the
reader and are not permitted to be
used to make accessories for sale,
however small the business.

foreword

Throughout the eras featured in this book, accessories have offered the best way to update fashions from one season to the next and in many cases have defined the look of the decade. Styles have ranged from classic to imaginative, blending colourful fabrics with whimsical shapes, created from a wide selection of materials influenced by the social and economic climate of the times.

For decades, accessories have offered an economical and inventive way to create a new look or complete an outfit. During the Second World War, for example, when clothing was rationed and women were encouraged to 'make do and mend' what they already had, accessories were easy to fashion from small leftover scraps of fabric or old pre-loved pieces of clothing.

Today fashion accessories are big business and, coupled with the current resurgence in interest in the home-sewing industry, alongside a hankering for all things vintage, *Making Vintage Accessories* offers a comprehensive selection of sewing patterns designed by the author and influenced by the styles of bygone eras. It also serves as a guide to making those essential fashion finishing touches, guiding the home-sewer through how to make an array of easy and inventive vintage-style sewn accessories from small scraps of fabric. Patterns are included for eight handbags, five hats and a selection of scarves, tippets, belts and stitched jewellery items.

The book also gives tips on how to interpret genuine vintage accessory patterns for use with modern-day fabrics. The first section of the book explains techniques and fabrics, the main body details the 25 projects, and the back section gives the pattern templates for the projects ready to photocopy and use. There are also pictures of how to wear the finished items.

Emma Brennan

contents

1920s

mabel
page 32

vita
page 36

louisa
page 40

beatrice
page 45

clementine
page 48

1930s

katherine
page 54

eleanor
page 58

jessica
page 63

deborah
page 66

diana
page 70

1940s

agatha
page 76

lauren
page 80

annie
page 84

celia
page 89

ivy
page 92

1950s

connie
page 98

iris
page 102

molly
page 107

stella
page 110

sylvia
page 114

1960s

cynthia
page 120

sophia
page 124

daphne
page 128

jean
page 133

marianne
page 136

materials and **techniques**

This section explains the basic materials and the main techniques you need to create the 25 accessory projects in this book. Using the pattern templates, choosing fabrics, base materials, making handles and fixing fastenings are all covered in step-by-step instructions that take you through the assembly stages of sample accessories.

In the next section of the book, the projects have detailed step-by-step instructions, and are illustrated with pictures where a technique is different from the standard methods outlined in this section. It is essential that you read and understand the methods outlined in each relevant introductory subject area before you go on to attempt an individual project.

Basic sewing techniques are not covered in the book, as it is assumed that the reader will have knowledge of rudimentary sewing skills. It is not necessary to be an expert, but you should be able to operate a sewing machine competently and have a good knowledge of basic hand stitches.

accessory-making essentials

To make the accessories in this book you will need the following equipment and materials:

- A paper pattern template copied from the book
- Fabric or materials listed for each project
- Sewing machine
- Iron
- Dressmaking pins (long quilting pins are best)
- Scissors (dressmaking)
- Needles
- Selection of threads
- Tape measure

also useful for some projects:

- Rotating hole punch (for leather/fabric)
- Jewellery-making pliers

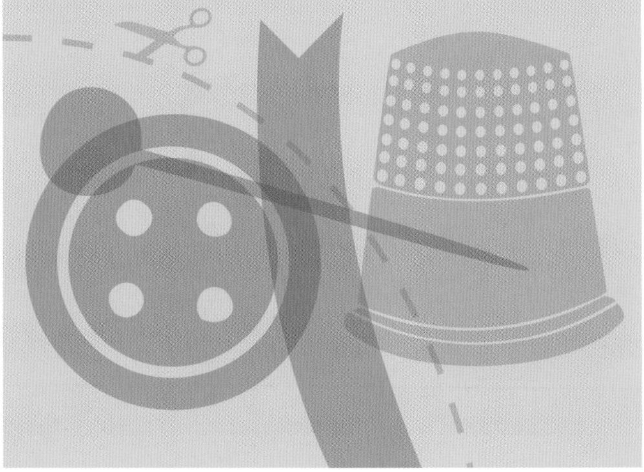

how to use the patterns in the book

This book contains the pattern templates to make each one of the 25 projects, ranging from bags and hats to belts and scarves. Patterns for all of the sewing projects are printed at the back of the book from page 140 onwards. Reproduced at a reduced size, they are designed to be enlarged using a photocopier, ensuring the black arrow on each page is placed in the top left corner of the photocopier and that the dotted rule is aligned with the top edge of the glass. The easiest way to do this is to take the book to a photocopy shop and get the pattern sheets enlarged onto A3 size paper following these instructions. The pattern pieces will then be the correct size to cut out and use straight away.

Where the same pattern pieces are used for two bag styles, the templates have clear directions for both. Most pattern pieces have been drawn 'on the fold' (see below), so the piece needs to be cut on the fold of the fabric or redrawn on the fold of a larger piece of paper (if you prefer) before use. This enables pattern pieces for larger handbags to be included in the book. I have tried to limit the styles to sizes that can easily be enlarged on standard size A3 photocopy paper.

to cut out your accessory

First enlarge the relevant pattern templates and cut them out. Lay the pattern pieces onto the fabric following the directions given in the project. You should then pin the pattern pieces onto the fabric and cut around them with dressmaking scissors.

Where a pattern template has **fold line** written along an edge, this means you must place this edge of the pattern along a fold in the fabric when you are cutting out the accessory. In effect, the template is 'half' of the piece – by cutting on the fold you will cut out the other half at the same time. This also has its advantages in ensuring that each piece is cut symmetrically. The instructions for each project will remind you when a piece needs to be cut on the fold. Some people prefer to redraw the template with the 'on fold' edge along the folded edge of a larger piece of paper to make the pattern piece full size before cutting the fabric.

Remember to enlarge all pattern pieces by 200%

sewing tip

Note that the relevant **seam allowances** have already been added to the patterns in this book and are approx. ½in (13mm) unless otherwise stated.

and techniques

11

materials

basic stitches

Most of the sewing in this book is completed with a sewing machine, using a standard sewing machine foot. Unless otherwise stated, a regular-length straight stitch is used. At the beginning and end of each seam, you must make a few backstitches in order to secure the seam. A zigzag stitch is also used in some of the projects for neatening edges.

There are a few hand-stitches used in several of the projects in the book (**A**).

zigzag stitch

A machine zigzag stitch is used in projects to neaten the raw edges of fabric that might fray (on the inside of hats, for example) or as a decorative feature on scarves.

gathering stitch

A gathering stitch is used on the centre of bows and trims. This is a basic running stitch that is pulled up to form gathers. It is advisable to use a double thickness of thread for this stitch.

slip stitch

Many of the projects have a gap in the lining through which the bag, scarf or belt is turned right side out. In this case, you will be instructed to slip stitch the opening closed (**B**). This means that you should hand-stitch the opening neatly to avoid a bulky or untidy seam, especially where visible.

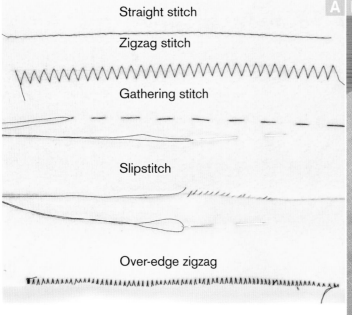

Straight stitch

Zigzag stitch

Gathering stitch

Slipstitch

Over-edge zigzag

A B

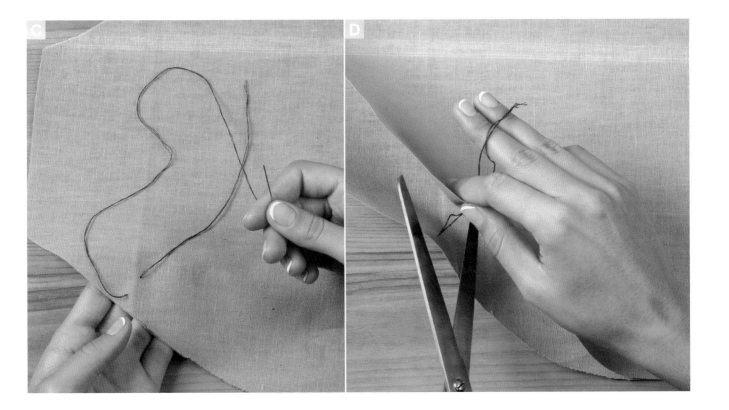

tailor's tacks

For most of the projects in the book, it is possible to transfer the marker points for pleats and fasteners from the paper patterns onto the cut fabric using pins or a soft pencil. When this in not appropriate, especially when transferring markers to a double thickness of fabric, you can use tailor's tacks. To make these, thread a needle with a long double thickness of thread. Use a colour that will show up well against your fabric. Make a stitch through both layers of fabric at the marker point, in and out (**C**). Cut the thread leaving two tails around 3in (8cm) in length. Take off the pattern piece. Carefully separate the two layers of fabric and snip the threads between the layers (**D**). This will leave a thread marker at the same point on both pieces of fabric.

fabrics

One of the great things about making accessories is that you can use up pieces of leftover fabric from bigger projects or you can treat yourself to a small piece of special fabric and add a colourful splash or statement to an outfit. The beauty is that you can make fashion accessories out of virtually any fabric. Of course, some are more suitable for different types of accessory than others, as detailed below.

The fabric you use to create a vintage-style fashion accessory does not have to be vintage itself. There are many vintage-style fabrics on the market today with nostalgic, retro prints or modern-day alternatives to vintage staples such as velvet and wool.

Consider furnishing fabrics for bags, hats and belts. Many of these will not require an interfacing (see pages 16–17). For scarves it is better to choose soft draping fabrics such as silks and velveteen. Colour is a very important factor, too. Choosing fabrics in muted or faded colours can really add to the vintage look. Of course, if you have a piece of vintage lace or a small scrap of vintage fabric that is not big enough to make an entire scarf or bag, you can incorporate this into an accessory – perhaps as a flap on a bag or a trim on a pair of customized gloves.

For the projects in this book, I have used a variety of fabrics from the traditional, such as wool tweeds for day bags, to more lavish textiles, such as faux fur for collars and hat bands and velvet for evening wear. Below, I describe some of the fabrics I have used and their special qualities for making accessories.

wool tweed

Wool tweed is one of my favourite fabrics because it is traditional yet is now produced in some wonderful modern weaves and patterns incorporating a whole spectrum of colours. Wool takes on a natural hue when dyed. Tweed can be soft yet hardwearing, making it ideal for use in bag or hat projects and as backings for scarves, collars and belts. I find it easy to work with and it produces a polished finish with a rustic edge. See the suppliers section (pages 186–7) for sources of tweed.

polar fleece

Fleece is a very modern fabric and although originally intended for use in sports and outdoor clothing, it is extremely versatile and has many qualities that make it ideal for a range of other items, such as accessories. I have used it in this book to make hats, scarves and glove trims. I love the idea that I have developed hats from a vintage idea or shape and used them with such a modern fabric. It is great for hats because of the stretch (**A**), which helps overcome sizing issues. However, fleece is usually more stretchy one way than it is the other. I would always advise hats be cut with the band along the *least* stretchy grain. If not, it can stretch too far and end up too big! Other qualities I love

Generally, fake fur should be cut with the pattern pieces reversed and laying on the back (non-furry side) of the fabric. Try to get the scissors in between the fur pile rather than cutting 'through'. And don't forget to have a vacuum cleaner ready to pick up any of the stray bits! When you have sewn a seam with fake fur, pick the fur out of the finished seams with a blunt bodkin or needle. Pin pieces together with pins at right angles to the edge and leave pins in while you sew to avoid the fabric or lining 'walking'.

leather

This is only used for a couple of projects in the book. Many people are nervous of using leather because it is expensive and traditionally regarded as quite difficult to sew. I have experimented over the years with roller and Teflon feet but I have come up with a method that works for me, used in **Stella** (pages 110–13). I cut out the pieces in leather, felt and fusible web (such as Heat and Bond). Iron the fusible web piece onto the felt piece. Peel the backing paper off, then place the leather and felt sections wrong sides together. Iron the two pieces together from the felt side through a cloth. Doing this means that the leather doesn't get damaged and you can then sew it with the felt side up. This avoids the leather sticking to the foot and means you can use a standard foot and needle on your machine.

about fleece are that it does not fray, it has the cosy appearance of wool when made up and it is generally not difficult to sew.

fake (faux) fur

This is used to make some of the tippets and collars in the projects as well as the crowns on hats. Fake furs have really come on a pace in recent years and do look like the real thing rather than 'toy' fur. Real fur was used a lot in the 1920s and 30s. Thankfully fake fur is now much better and more durable than the real thing and it is one of those fabrics that instantly adds vintage appeal and a touch of glamour to an accessory design.

structure and suitable base materials for bags and hats

Handmade bags and hats that are fashioned on a home sewing machine will not have the structure of a factory-produced equivalent but, to me, that is part of the appeal. Particularly in the war years, it was not possible to obtain the materials needed to create a polished finish. In my opinion, the slightly homemade, one-off look adds to the period feel.

quilted calico

There are many options for base materials for making handbags, hats and belts, into which I am not going to go into too much detail. For the purpose of this book, I have used quilted calico as a base material or interfacing for all of the bags and hats (**A**). This consists of wadding or batting that has been quilt-stitched onto calico. It is available in shops that sell quilting fabrics and supplies. I use quilted calico in all of my own projects because it is firm, holds its shape and gives substance to the accessory without adding stiffness. If you cannot find quilted calico or if you would rather use a different type of interfacing, you can substitute it for one of the alternatives.

iron-on or fusible interfacing

These are usually only suitable for fabrics which can be ironed at fairly high temperatures. Brands such as Vilene, which are made from non-woven synthetic fibres, are readily available in a variety of weights and are easy to use. They are used in this book for flaps on bags, to stiffen belts and on some hat pieces.

sew-in craft weight or pelmet interfacing

This is a durable material that can have a soft or hard feel. It adds weight and structure and can be used with most fabrics, as it doesn't have to be ironed on. It has to be stitched to the main fabric before the project is assembled and it can be used instead of quilted calico. This material is useful when you wish to achieve a more defined shape.

wadding

This is a soft but lofty material that adds bulk and padding without stiffness. Wadding is usually sewn in, although there are now some fusible brands on the market. Substitute wadding for quilted calico if you wish to achieve a softer look.

Other interlinings not used in the book include buckram or canvas materials – these are more expensive to use as interfacing fabrics but they are long lasting, durable and give a tailored look.

plastic canvas

This is plastic mesh which is used for cross-stitch. It is used in the book for cutting out a 'base' rectangle to insert in the bottom of a bag. It gives shape and a firm base to the project. Thick cardboard or plastic can be used instead.

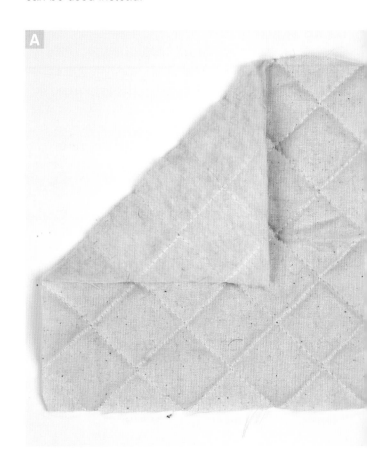

A

piece preparation

Interfacing pieces for accessories should be stitched or fused to the relevant fabric pieces *before* assembly. Remember to use only fusible (iron-on) interfacings on fabric pieces that are made of cotton or other suitable fabrics. Do not use fusible interfacings on fake leather or suede. These synthetic fabrics often cannot be ironed and, even if you do manage to successfully fuse the interfacing to the fabric, it invariably comes unstuck over time. Ironing interfacing onto velvet will also crush the pile.

iron-on interfacing

Before you start assembling your project, attach interfacing to all of the relevant pieces. If you are using a fabric that is compatible with fusible interfacing, you can simply iron the fusible interfacing pieces onto the reverse side of the fabric. It is often necessary to use a little steam or a damp cloth to help release the bonding unit in the interfacing. Ensure that the interfacing is completely stuck down all over, particularly around the edges.

sew-in interfacing

If your fabric is not compatible with iron-on interfacing, you must baste-stitch the relevant accessory pieces to the interfacing pieces before you start assembling the item. As mentioned before, I have used quilted calico as an interlining for all of the bags and hats in this book.

Step 1

First lay the interfacing pieces on the reverse side of the corresponding fabric pieces. Pin from the right side, using pins at right angles to the raw edge so that they can be left in while machine-basting. (This will avoid the need to hand-baste, but if you feel more comfortable hand-basting, you can do so). Smooth out any wrinkles as you pin.

Step 2

Using a long stitch length, machine-baste the fabric and interfacing together around the entire outside edge of each piece. Use a seam allowance of about ½in (13mm) from the outside edge. If you stitch from the interfacing side, this will help to avoid the fabric puckering or moving as you stitch (**A**).

sewing tip

Before you start any bag project, make sure you have transferred all relevant pleat, snap or other marker points onto the cut pieces.

fasteners

If you are making a bag, you will usually need to attach the fastener to the relevant lining or bag pieces *after* you have attached the interfacing and *before* you start assembling the bag. Most of the bags in this book use magnetic snap fasteners, while the belts and tippets use a mix of Velcro, big traditional snap fasteners and buttons. I have purposely avoided zips in order to keep all of the construction methods as simple as possible.

magnetic snaps

Magnetic snaps are the first choice of fastener for modern handbags because they are easy to use, simple to apply and invisible from the outside. Available in a range of sizes and metal colour finishes, they are ideal for use with flaps or 'touch-and-close' style bags.

A magnetic snap has four components (**A**). One half of the snap is magnetic, the other metal half clicks into the centre of the magnet to snap it shut. There are also two backing discs with holes in the centre, which sit on the other side of the fabric. The 'teeth' on the back of the snaps are pushed through holes in the fabric then through these backing discs. The teeth are then bent back in an outward direction thus securing the fastener. To stabilize the fabric and give the snap a secure base, it is advisable to insert a small piece of craft interfacing between the back of the fabric and the backing disc.

how to apply a magnetic snap

Step 1
Transfer the magnetic snap position marks on the pattern piece onto the relevant interfaced fabric piece – where possible onto the interfacing side – using a chalk pencil or felt pen. Make two small holes through both thicknesses (fabric and interfacing) using a leather hole punch if you have one, at the marker positions – they will be about ½in (13mm) apart.

Step 2
Push the teeth of the 'non-magnetic' half of the clasp through the hole from the right side of the fabric, so that the snap part sits on the fabric side. This will be on the right side of the under part of the flap if you are making a bag with a flap, or on the right side of the inside facing/lining if making a touch-and-close bag (**B**).

Step 3
Make two small holes in the centre of the snap stabilizer squares (2in/5cm sq of craft interfacing), about ½in (13mm) apart. Push the teeth of the snap through the holes in the snap stabilizer also. Put the backing disc of the snap over the teeth and bend the teeth outwards using pliers, so that this half of the snap is secure.

Step 4
Fix the other half of the snap in the same way.

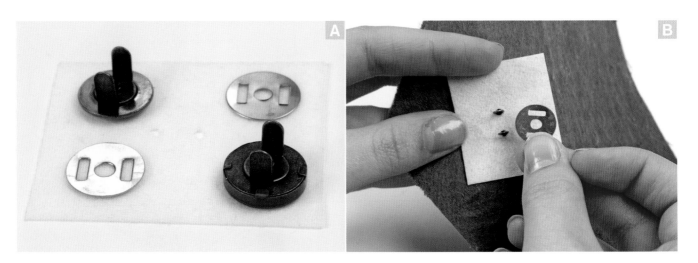

velcro – an alternative to the magnetic snap

Velcro is not a very vintage fastening, but it does the job! If you cannot find magnetic snaps, it can be used as an alternative on bags. It is also a good choice as a fastener on collars and belts. Although it can now be purchased in some different colours, limited ranges mean that it is often not possible to match it perfectly to your fabric. Where possible, do use an exact match. Otherwise, black, white or neutral colours are best. It should generally only be used where it will not be seen from the outside.

Velcro has two parts – one of these parts has tiny hooks on it and the other half has loops. The two halves 'stick' together and can be pulled apart with ease. Velcro is suitable for use with touch-and-close style bags, where each half of the fastener is fixed onto the lining or facing on the inside of the bag, opposite one another (as with the magnetic snaps). Velcro is fairly easy to apply. Transfer the snap markers on the pattern pieces to the right side of the relevant fabric facing or lining piece. Place the Velcro centrally over the markers, pin and stitch all round the outside of each piece using a short stitch length.

assembling the bag

Once the front and back pieces of the bag have been interfaced and any relevant snap fasteners attached, you can start to assemble the bag (**C**). For bags that have a more three-dimensional shape, you will have to fold the lower corners of the bag to form a gusset.

Step 1
Pin the two interfaced front/back sections right sides together. Stitch round the sides and lower edges leaving a ½in (13mm) seam allowance (**D**). Clip the seams on any curved edges.

Step 2
If the bag has a gusset, fold the lower corners of the bag, matching seams, and pin/baste in place (**E**).

Step 3
Stitch straight across the lower corners to form a gusset. Repeat on the opposite corner (**F**).

Step 4
Turn the bag right side out (**G**) and press.

handles

Handbag handles need to be made and stitched to the bag before it is lined. You can either use commercially produced bag handles or you can make your own. Most of the bags in this book use handmade, flat-stitched handles in keeping with the homemade, vintage feel of the projects. However, if you wish, you can substitute the handle in each pattern for a commercial handle, which come in all shapes, sizes and colours (**A**). I have described below how to make a handle carrier and attach it to the bag.

self-fabric handles

I prefer to make handles that do not require turning. The following method can be applied to all kinds of fabric, and is used for most of the bags in this book.

Step 1
First cut out the fabric strip for each handle according to the template or measurements given in the pattern. Cut out iron-on interfacing the same size and iron it onto the reverse side of the handle piece. Fold the handle in half lengthways and press (**B**).

Step 2
Next, fold in the long edges of the fabric handle strip to the centre fold on each side, so that they meet in the middle (**C**) and press along both long folded edges.

Step 3
Now refold the handle in half lengthways down the initial centre fold and pin (**D**). Machine-stitch it together down the unfolded edge (**E**). You can also stitch again down the opposite long edge if you wish. With this method, the handle will end up being one quarter of the width of the original fabric strip.

attaching long handles to bags

When stitching handles to bags they must be attached to the main bag before the lining is joined to it. Attach handles with raw edges even and facing downwards (**F**). When the bag is lined, the handle will be sandwiched in between the lining and the bag and will then face upwards.

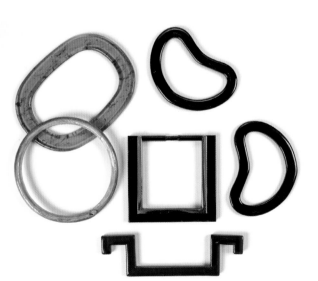

handle carriers

If you are using a purchased handle as in **Agatha** (page 76), or a circular handle, you will need to make a handle carrier with which to attach the handle to the bag. Some handles have detachable bars so that you can slip them onto the handle carrier after the bag has been assembled. Most, however, are solid and need to be attached to the bag via a handle carrier before the bag is lined. Some can be a little awkward to sew around and this is why is it imperative to leave a good seam allowance at the lower edge of the carrier to make it easier to access the top of the bag with the sewing machine.

Step 1

Measure around the handle to work out the depth and width of the handle carrier you need to make. Take the first measurement across the handle. When you have established the finished width carrier you require, double the measurement and add another 1in (25mm) to that measurement for seam allowances (½in/13mm each side). For example, if you wanted the carrier 2in (5cm) wide, cut it 5in (13cm) wide (twice 2in/5cm plus 1in/25mm seam allowance).

Step 2

For the other measurement (wrapped around the handle) you should measure loosely around the handle and add 2in (5cm) for seam allowance plus ease, depending on how thick the handle is and whether or not it unscrews. If it unscrews, you can attach the handle to the carrier after the bag is assembled, which makes it easier to turn the bag right side out.

Step 3

Iron interfacing to the reverse of the handle carrier. Stitch the two short ends together to form a tube. Turn right side out (**G**).

Step 4

Wrap around handle and with two raw edges even stitch together about ¼in (6mm) from the raw edge (**H**).

Step 5

To attach the handle carrier to the bag, make sure that you leave enough of a seam allowance for adequate stitching room. Pin to bag with the raw edges of the carrier even with raw upper edge of bag (**I**) and baste-stitch in place.

lining

Try to be inventive with bag linings. If you are using a plain fabric for the outside of the bag, try using a colourful or patterned toning fabric for the lining. Use silks for evening bags that will not receive hard wear and tear and use more durable cotton or nylon linings for day bags that will be used frequently.

In this book, all of the bags are lined in the same way using the basic 'pull-through' method. All of the bags are top opening and some have flaps. I have only included facings on one of the projects – most are all lined to the top for ease of making.

to line the bags in this book

Step 1

Take two lining pieces. Remember that if you are sewing in a label or using a magnetic snap, you will need to attach these before you sew the lining into the bag. Also, if you are adding an internal pocket, this will need to be stitched to the lining before you assemble it.

Step 2

Pin and stitch the lining pieces with the right sides together at the sides and lower edges, leaving an opening of around ¾in (2cm) in the centre of the lower edge. You will be 'turning' the bag through this opening (**A**). Stitch seams with a ¾in (2cm) seam allowance instead of the usual ½in (13mm) used for main pieces. This will make the lining slightly smaller than the bag so that it will sit inside the bag correctly, without puckering.

Step 3

Stitch corner gussets if appropriate (as for main bag instructions).

Step 4

Insert the bag into the lining and, with the right sides together, pin the lining to the bag (over the flap or handles if you have them) with the upper edges even. Stitch around the upper edge of the bag with a ¾in (2cm) seam allowance through all thicknesses, using a medium- to long-stitch length (**B**). Note that, depending on which kind of fabric you are using, there will be quite a lot of thicknesses to sew through (main fabric, interfacing, lining, flap, handle), so be sure to stitch very slowly and carefully. Trim the seam back

to around ½in (13mm) to eliminate bulk, and clip the seam allowance every inch or so, especially near the side seams of the bag.

Step 5

Now you must 'turn' the bag right side out by pulling it through the opening in the bottom of the lining (**C**). Slip stitch or machine-stitch the opening in the lining and then turn the lining to the inside of the bag. Roll the lining with your fingers so that it is not visible from the outside and pin in place all round the top, ensuring that everything sits correctly (**D**). Topstitch through all layers, about ½in (13mm) from the top of the bag. Use a long stitch length and sew cautiously through the bulkier areas (**E**). Press lightly.

Step 6

If necessary, to secure the lining inside the bag further, you can also hand-stitch a few stitches at the side seams, through the bag and facings, invisibly in the 'ditch' of the seam. Give a final press.

pockets

Some of the projects in this book have internal pockets. Although pockets in vintage bags were small – often just big enough to house a mirror or handkerchief – these days, people usually require pockets for mobile phones, diaries, keys and other 'essentials' of modern living! You can add a pocket to the inside or outside of any of the bags quite easily, by adapting one of the techniques detailed in **Agatha** (page 76) and **Cynthia** (page 120). If you are a more experienced sewer, you can add a zippered pocket or put a button, snap or flap on the pocket for added security.

hats

With hats there are some general rules to bear in mind that apply to all styles. The main issue with hats is sizing as, unlike a bag, a hat has to fit. Head sizes can vary by up to 2in (5cm). Although I have sized all hats in this book to fit a fairly standard 22in (56cm) head, soft fabric hats such as those included in the book can be made slightly larger by using smaller seams on panels or made slightly smaller by pulling in the grosgrain ribbon tighter, adding a piece of elastic under the ribbon at the back, or sewing with bigger seams.

Original 1940s hat patterns I have bought often gave advice on adjusting hats to a larger or smaller head size. Although hat patterns were sold in individual sizes, the patterns stated that you could adjust them to fit a head ½in (13mm) smaller or larger. This is the recommendation in a 1940s McCall pattern for hats and bags:

'Cut material according to pattern and cutting layouts. To adjust hats to a larger or smaller head size, join ribbon headband to fit your correct head size. Join seam of crown sections starting at upper edge (using ½in seam allowance), gradually slanting the seam allowance to ⅜in for a larger size or ⅝in for a smaller size.'

Several of the hats in this book are made using polar fleece, which is stretchy and helps overcome some of these sizing issues. Traditionally, the crown of a hat made from non-stretch materials should be cut on the bias (cross grain) of the fabric to give a little more stretch. As a general rule, pin the back seam in the crown or hatband and try it on first. If it is going to be too big, then stitch it with a bigger seam allowance. If you are using fleece, you can stretch or ease the other pieces to fit to the band. With hats from non-stretch fabrics, as in the advice from the McCall pattern, you can taper the seam toward the top in order to overcome any possible problems fitting the top to the crown.

I have finished most of the hats in the book with grosgrain ribbon. I find it easiest to pin this around the inside of the hat and then try the hat on. If it is still a little large, re-pin easing in more fullness (i.e., using a shorter length of ribbon).

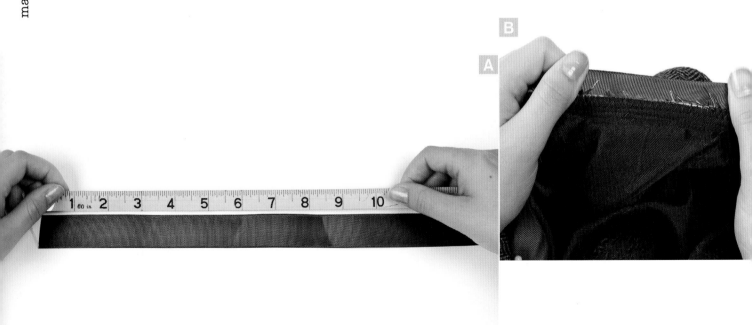

fitting grosgrain ribbon inside a hat

Step 1
Measure the grosgrain to fit snugly but comfortably around your head and add a 2in (5cm) seam allowance for overlap and fold, at the end (**A**).

Step 2
Once you have assembled the hat, you can zigzag-stitch around the inside raw edges to prevent any fraying before you stitch the grosgrain ribbon on (**B**).

Step 3
Next pin the ribbon to the hat covering the seam and zigzagging. Fold one end of the ribbon over and overlap the two ribbon ends with the folded edge on top (**C**).

Step 4
Finally stitch the ribbon into place about ¼in (6mm) from the upper edge of the grosgrain (**D**). Hand- or machine-stitch the folded end of the grosgrain ribbon in place.

Step 5
If using fake fur, pick the fur out of the seam at the upper and lower edges of the crown using a blunt needle or bodkin (**E**).

belts

Belts had their heyday in the 1930s but they remained a fashion staple throughout the 20th century and still feature in fashion collections almost every season. Belts can be made from a variety of materials depending on whether you want to achieve a firm or soft finish.

Sizing is of course an issue with belts. The belts in this book have been made in one size but each project gives information on altering the size of the belt to fit different girths. Belts such as Jean, which is tied with a scarf, allow a little leeway for sizing, whereas shaped belts, such as **Stella** (page 110), need to be made either to sit on the hips or round the waist to fit.

scarves and collars

Some of the scarf projects in this book use a large rectangle of fabric. Where this is too big to include a pattern piece, I have given measurements to cut to instead, in addition to the pattern pieces required for the other components of the scarf.

The collars are offered in one size, but each project gives details on how to adjust the sizing to fit.

embellishments

I have included a project in each decade's chapter that I have loosely termed as 'jewellery' but which are primarily 'trim' ideas that can be used for jewellery making or as trims for accessories or clothing. Some of the other projects are trimmed with these items and some of the projects have their own embellishment details, which can also be swapped to another project.

Do not be afraid to mix and match the trims and even the accessories from two or more eras. You will be surprised how well they all blend with each other to create new and interesting looks.

genuine vintage patterns

With the growth of home and internet shopping, genuine vintage patterns are becoming much more widely accessible.

Many original patterns are very old and frail and can be very costly to buy. Some companies are now acquiring patterns on which the copyright has expired and are reissuing them at a smaller cost. Most of these patterns are literally reprints of the originals and therefore do not have instructions that are relevant to today's fabrics and techniques. The patterns can be useful for ideas on construction, piece shape and styling, but most have to be adapted to make them easier to work with. The suppliers list on page 186 shows a few internet companies that sell original vintage patterns.

Here are some things to bear in mind when working with vintage patterns. The copyright still exists on patterns that were printed after 1930 so the designs are not free for use by designers to simply copy. Also bear in mind that the fabrics used as stiffeners are outdated now and there are good modern alternatives. If you are using a vintage pattern, you can usually substitute interlining materials listed in the 'material required' section such as muslin and buckram for modern interfacings.

A commonly mentioned interlining is tarlatan, which is a starched, open-weave fabric, a bit like cheese cloth. Often hats and bags were made with the fabric layer on top, a layer of sheet cotton or flannelette sandwiched in between and a layer of tarlatan on the underside. By using quilted calico – which has a layer of wadding (batting) and a layer of calico stitched together – the texture of the finished item is similar to what you would have achieved with the vintage recommendations. You can of course just use a standard modern interfacing instead. Where 'crinoline' is mentioned (a stiff fabric of horse-hair and cotton or linen thread) this will usually have to be substituted for a firmer interfacing.

You will find that the instructions included in vintage patterns are quite scant. Several of the patterns I have bought for my own collection have the instructions for making two bags and two hat styles all printed on one side of A3 paper! Sometimes a page of 'general directions' was included, giving instructions on things such as adjusting patterns to fit different head sizes and finishing techniques. It is important to remember that more people sewed in the 1930s and 40s and a good knowledge of dressmaking and construction was assumed by pattern makers.

Take a good look at the methods used to construct the accessories, though. Some of the hats were not lined and in virtually all of pre-1960s bag patterns I have purchased, the linings are sewn into the bags by hand. You will notice that there was generally a lot more hand-stitching involved in patterns from the 1930s, 40s and 50s. Look at the ways I have constructed some of my patterns in the book. See if you can work out a way to assemble the pieces in a vintage pattern in a more modern, 'machine-friendly' way, simply by changing the order of construction.

Also look at ways of incorporating modern fasteners or handles. Always plan the best way to construct an accessory first and make a list of the sequence of steps. Make detailed notes as you go along and keep these with the vintage pattern. Try to avoid writing on the vintage pattern pieces or instructions themselves, as this will reduce the value of the pattern should you wish to sell it on.

making **vintage** accessories

1920s

bag dimensions

Approximately 9in (23cm) tall
(excluding handle) by 10in
(26cm) wide; handle 16in
(41cm) long

pattern pieces

pages 140–3

suggested fabrics

for bag top and bottom:
Wool flannel/tweed in two
contrasting colours

for lining:
Firm weight silk or cotton

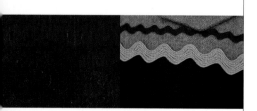

mabel

1920s RICKRACK TRIMMED OVAL BAG

**Bags in the early 1920s tended to be quite small, so I have
created this cute little oval-shaped bag to be deceptively roomy
but neat enough to use for evening or special occasion wear.
The rickrack trim and bold green and black colours are also
evocative of the period.**

This bag features a small
flap that is perfect for
displaying an impressive
trim. In order to tie in with the
flat rickrack on the front and
back of the bag, I have made a

decorative rickrack flower, as in
Clementine, pages 48–51, but
you could always pin a bejewelled
antique brooch to the flap for a
more decadent feel.

you will need

✱ 9in (23cm) of wool fabric, 36in
(92cm) wide for top of bag and flap

✱ 10in (26cm) of contrasting wool
fabric 36in (92cm) wide for bag
bottom and handle

✱ 24in (61cm) of jumbo rickrack

✱ 22in (56cm) of medium rickrack

✱ 12in (31cm) of lining fabric, 36in
(92cm) wide for bag lining

✱ 12in (31cm) of quilted calico, 36in
(92cm) wide for bag interfacing

✱ piece of iron-on interfacing 5in
(13cm) x 30in (76cm) for handle
and flap

✱ piece of plastic canvas or stiff
card, 6in (15cm) x 2in (5cm) for
base of bag

✱ 1 magnetic snap fastener

for flower on flap

✱ 18in (46cm) of jumbo rickrack for
flower outer

✱ 12in (31cm) of medium rickrack
for flower inner

✱ 1 vintage glass button for flower
centre

cutting out

✱ Cut 2 x piece **A** (top front/back)
on fold from main fabric 1

✱ Cut 2 x piece **B** (lower front/
back) on fold from main fabric 2

✱ Cut 2 x piece **C** (flap) on fold
from main fabric 1

✱ Cut 2 x piece **C** (flap) on fold
from iron-on interfacing

✱ Cut 2 x piece **D** (bag lining) on
fold from lining fabric

✱ Cut 2 x piece **D** (bag lining) on
fold from quilted calico interfacing

✱ Cut 1 x piece **E** (handle) on fold
from main fabric 2

✱ Cut 1 x piece **E** (handle) on fold
from iron-on interfacing

making up instructions

Step 1

With right sides together, pin and stitch lower and upper front/back pieces **A** and **B** together along edges marked with dotted line on pattern pieces leaving a ½in (13mm) seam allowance (**A**). Press seam open flat.

Step 2

Pin assembled bag front/back to corresponding front/back quilted-calico interfacing pieces **D**, and baste together round entire outside edge (**B**). Refer to **Sew-in Interfacing**, page 17.

Step 3

On interfaced front/back sections, stitch row of medium rickrack 1in (25mm) above seam line (**C**). Stitch a row of jumbo rickrack covering the seam.

Step 4

Transfer magnetic snap position marker onto bag front. Fix the magnetic half. See **How to Apply a Magnetic Snap**, page 18.

Step 5

Pin the two front/back pieces right sides together. Stitch together at side and lower edges, leaving the corners free. Then fold lower corners of the bag, matching seams, and stitch straight across to form a gusset. For help with this step refer to **Assembling the Bag**, page 19. Clip seam allowance along curved edge, turn bag right side out and press lightly.

Step 6

Iron interfacing onto reverse side of handle piece **E** and fold in long raw edges to centre. Fold handle in half lengthways and topstitch together down open side and again along closed side, approx ¼in (6mm) from edges. Refer to **Self-fabric Handles**, page 20.

Step 7

On outside, positioned centred over side seams with raw edges even, pin handle to bag and baste in place – refer to **Attaching Long Handles to Bags**, page 20.

Step 8

Iron interfacing onto the wrong side of both flap pieces **C**. Transfer the magnetic snap position marker onto the flap underside piece and fix the non-magnetic half of the snap (**D**). Refer to **How to Apply a Magnetic Snap**, page 18. Stitch flap pieces right sides together around the sides and lower edges. Clip corners and turn right side out (**E**). Press and topstitch approx ¼in (6mm) from the edge.

Step 9

Pin the finished flap to the back of bag centrally, right outside of flap against right outside of bag back, having raw edges even. Baste using a long stitch length, approx ½in (13mm) from the edge.

Step 10

Stitch front and back lining pieces **D** together (having right sides together) at side and lower edges, leaving corners free. Leave a gap of about 4in (10cm) in the seam

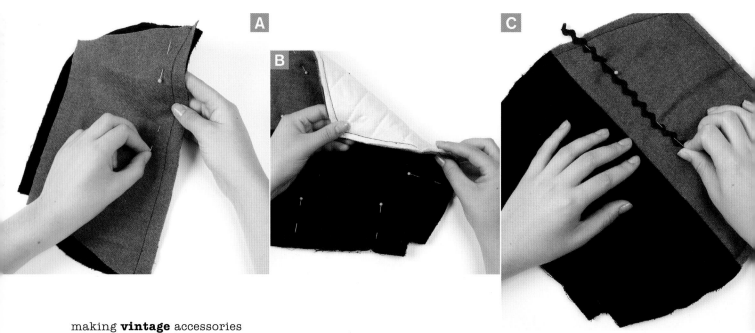

at the bottom for turning the bag through. Fold the lower corners of the bag matching seams and stitch straight across to form gusset.

Step 11

Insert bag into lining with right sides together. Pin bag and lining together through all thicknesses round upper edges, having raw edges even. Stitch through all thicknesses using a normal stitch length, leaving a seam allowance of just over ½in (13mm). Trim seam back to ⅜in (1cm) and clip into the seam allowance at sides.

Step 12

Turn the bag right side out through the opening in the bottom of the lining and push the lining to the inside of the bag. Refer to **To Line the Bags in this Book**, page 22. Roll the lining with your fingers so that it is not visible from the outside and pin it in place all round top, ensuring that the flap will sit correctly. Topstitch through all

variations

This bag could be made using a plain fabric for the bottom part and a patterned or floral print for the top half and flap for spring or summer. For a more pieced or patchworked look, try using different and contrasting prints and plains for every section of the bag.

The pattern pieces are not very big, so this bag offers an ideal way to use up all the small treasured scraps of fabric you might have stashed away.

layers, about ½in (13mm) from the top of the bag, using a long stitch length.

Step 13

Insert a piece of plastic canvas or thick card into the bottom of the bag through the opening to give shape to the base of the bag. Slip stitch the opening in the lining closed, tuck lining back into bag and give the bag a final press under a cloth. Press first

with flap open and then again with flap closed. If necessary, in order to secure the lining into the bag further, you can hand-stitch a few stitches at the side seams, through bag and lining.

Step 14

Make a rickrack flower following the instructions in **Clementine**, pages 48–51. Hand-stitch in place on flap (**F**).

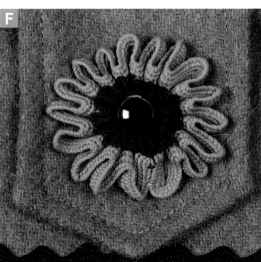

vita

1920s CLOCHE HAT WITH RICKRACK TASSEL TRIM

This hat is reminiscent of the cloche hats of the early 1920s. With a crown that gently widens toward the top and a neat brim that narrows toward the back, this style suits most face shapes. It makes a smart winter addition to any wardrobe and looks equally good in smart black fake fur for city chic or in rustic tweeds to suit country attire.

I have used fake fur for the crown to give it a more textured look. The brim and top are made from polar fleece and I have trimmed the crown with a detachable rickrack decoration featuring a tassel, also reminiscent of the 1920s.

hat dimensions

To fit a medium-size head measurement of approx 22in (56cm)

pattern pieces

A **B** **C**

pages 144–5

suggested fabrics

for crown:
fake fur

for top and brim:
fleece or tweed

for lining:
firm weight silk

you will need

* 9in (23cm) of fake fur fabric, 32in (82cm) wide for hat crown

* 18in (46cm) of fleece or tweed fabric, 45in (114cm) wide for brim and top

* 12in (31cm) of silk fabric, 45in (114cm) wide for lining

* 9in (23cm) of quilted calico, 32in (82cm) wide for interfacing crown

* 18in (46cm) of iron-on or sew-in interfacing, 45in (114cm) wide for interfacing brim and top

* approx 24in (61cm) of grosgrain ribbon, 1in (25mm) wide for band

for flower trim

* approx 18in (46cm) of jumbo rickrack for flower outer in two contrasting colours

* ⅞in (22mm) braid-covered button for centre

* tassel

* sew-on brooch bar

cutting out

* Cut 1 x piece **A** (crown) on fold from fake fur

* Cut 1 x piece **A** (crown) on fold from sew-in interfacing

* Cut 1 x piece **A** (crown) on fold from lining

* Cut 1 x piece **B** (top) on fold from fleece or tweed

* Cut 1 x piece **B** (top) on fold from iron-on or sew-in interfacing

* Cut 1 x piece **B** (top) on fold from lining

* Cut 2 x piece **C** (brim) on fold from fleece or tweed

* Cut 2 x piece **C** (brim) on fold from iron-on or sew-in interfacing

making up instructions

NB: I have not interfaced the crown in the step-by-step pictures, as the fur fabric was firm enough without.

Step 1

Stitch crown piece **A** to the corresponding crown interfacing piece. Refer to **Sew-in Interfacing**, page 17. With right sides together, stitch centre back seam in crown, leaving a ½in (13mm) seam allowance.

Step 2

Iron or stitch interfacing to wrong sides of hat top **B** and hat brim **C** pieces, again referring to **Sew-in Interfacing**, page 17, where necessary. Pin hat top to crown and stitch, leaving a ½in (13mm) seam allowance (**A**). Clip into the seam allowance all round (**B**), then turn it right side out (**C**).

Step 3

Stitch centre back seam in crown lining **A**, leaving a ½in (13mm) seam allowance. Pin top lining **B** to crown lining and stitch, leaving a ½in (13mm) seam allowance (**D**). With wrong sides together, pin lining crown/top inside hat crown/top matching centre back seams and keeping lower raw edges even (**E**). Stitch together about ½in (13mm) from the raw edge.

Step 4

Stitch centre back seam in both interfaced brim pieces. Pin brim sections right sides together with the centre back seams matching. Stitch the brims together around the outside edge, leaving a ½in (13mm) seam allowance (**F**). Clip into the seam allowance all round, then turn brim right side out.

Step 5

Pin and then topstitch brim approx. ½in (13mm) from outer seam and then again approx. ½in (13mm) from the first line of topstitching (**G**). Machine-baste inner open edges of brim together approx ½in (13mm) from the raw edge.

Step 6

Match centre back seam in lined hat crown/top with centre back seam in brim, and pin together, right outside of hat against upper side of brim with brim facing upward and raw edges even. Stitch leaving a ½in (13mm) seam allowance.

Step 7

Zigzag-stitch around the raw edges to prevent any fraying. Try the hat on to ascertain sizing. Pin grosgrain to the hat covering the seam and zigzagging (**H**).

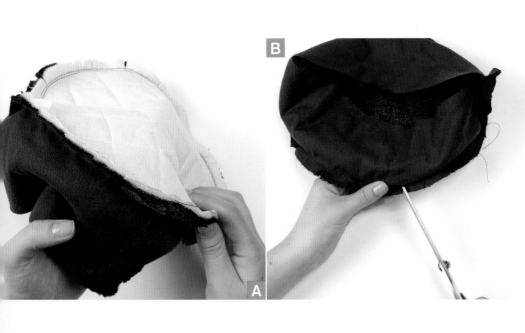

If the hat is a bit large, pin the grosgrain taking in a little of the fullness so the hat will be tighter.

Step 8

Fold one end of the ribbon over and overlap the two ends with folded edge on top. Stitch the ribbon in place about ¼in (6mm) from the upper edge of the grosgrain. Stitch the folded end of the grosgrain ribbon to itself. Turn the ribbon upwards and stitch with a few hand-stitches to the hat lining. For help with the above two stages, refer to **Hats**, page 25.

Step 9

Pick the fur out of the seams using a blunt needle or bodkin, referring to **Hats**, page 25 for help.

Step 10

Make a double rickrack chrysanthemum brooch with tassel trim as detailed in **Clementine**, pages 48–51, and pin in place to one side of the crown.

Try experimenting with different types of interfacing. Depending on which fabric you use for your hat, it may only be necessary to interface one of the brim sections. For example, for the brown version of the hat (below), I did not use an interfacing on the crown because the fabric was dense and stiff enough without. I used quilted calico to interface the hat top and one of the brim pieces. In general, iron-on interfacing tends to give a firmer feel, whereas quilted calico gives a loftier look without making the hat too stiff.

The type and amount of interfacing you use for the various components of this hat depends on the look you hope to achieve. Using iron-on interfacing to stiffen the brim will result in a more tailored look. If you need to interface any fake fur sections, use the sew-in variety as ironing the fur can squash the pile.

variations

An alternative hat in chocolate brown can be made using a flatter, astrakhan-type fur for the crown and smart herringbone wool tweed for the brim and top. You could use velvet instead of the tweed or you could try making a really big tweed rosette with a covered button centre for a variation on the country theme.

vita

39

1920s

E

F

G

H

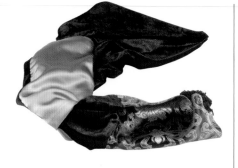

scarf dimensions

Approximately 58in (147cm)
long by 10in (26cm) wide

pattern pieces

pages 146–7

suggested fabrics

for main scarf:
soft velveteen

for pointed end:
patterned silk brocade

for tuck-through end:
plain soft satin or silk

louisa

1920s TUCK-THROUGH EVENING SCARF

Scarves are a simple accessory to make, with infinite possibilities for trims and countless ways to tie them. Believed to date back to Roman times, scarves were originally worn mostly by men, particularly in the 19th century when they took the form of the cravat.

By the 20th century and throughout the decades featured in this book, scarves became a staple fashion accessory in women's wardrobes, appearing in many forms, from short fur tippets to stunning long satin stoles. They have ranged from purely decorative, jaunty, knotted neckerchiefs to functional uses, such as being tied around the head turban style during the war years.

This scarf is designed to be worn loosely around the neck for evening wear, although the shape and style – with one end tucking through the other – could be replicated in soft wool or fleece for day wear.

you will need

✱ 24in (61cm) by 45in (114cm) of velveteen for main scarf

✱ 12in (31cm) of satin brocade, 30in (76cm) wide for pointed end

✱ 14in (36cm) of soft satin or silk, 36in (92cm) wide for tuck-through end

✱ One tassel to match, approx. 3½in (9cm) long

cutting out

✱ Cut 2 x piece **A** (scarf point panel) on fold from brocade silk

✱ Cut 2 x piece **B** (tuck-through panel) on fold from plain silk/satin

✱ Cut 1 rectangle of velvet 21in (53cm) wide by 45in (114cm) long for the main scarf

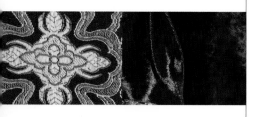

making up instructions

Step 1
First choose an interesting patterned brocade for the scarf point panel and remember to cut it out so that the design is central to the panel (**A**).

Step 2
Pin the two scarf point panel **A** pieces right sides together. Stitch together around both curved edges, leaving a ½in (13mm) seam allowance, and ideally leaving a tiny gap at the bottom of the point (between dots) for threading the tassel loop through (**B**). Pull the tassel loop through the gap. A crochet hook or bodkin can help with this. Hand-stitch the tassel loop in place from the wrong side of the scarf point.

Step 3
Clip the seam allowance at the curved edge of scarf point panel and turn right side out. Secure tassel further from the right side, stitching through the top a little to ensure that the tassel sits directly under the point without any loop showing (**C**).

Step 4
Stitch the two tuck-through panels **B** right sides together at side seams (marked with a broken line on the pattern template (**D**). Clip seams at corners of rectangle, then turn right sides out (**E**) and press at side seams. Fold the panel in half so that the two raw edges are even. Stitch together about ½in (13mm) from the raw edge (**F**).

Step 5
Pin the tuck-through panel to the main scarf at one short end. Position it ½in (13mm) from the raw edge on one side. Then fold the scarf over so that both raw edges of the main scarf are even and the tuck-through panel is now sandwiched in between in the fold. Pin and baste in place (**G**).

Step 6
Pin the pointed end panel to the main scarf at the other short end. Position it ½in (13mm) from the raw edge on one side. Fold the scarf over so that both raw edges of the main scarf are even and the pointed panel is sandwiched in between in the fold. Pin and baste in place.

Step 7

Stitch folded scarf (with end panels now basted sandwiched between) together along short end with tuck-through down long side seam, leaving a gap of about 3in (8cm) at the centre of the scarf for turning through. Continue the side seam the other side of the gap, and along the short end with the pointed panel. **NB: Take care not to catch the corners of the tuck through in the seam – it helps to pin the corners over out of the way before stitching the main seams.**

Step 8

Turn the scarf right side out through the gap you left, hand-stitch the gap closed and press the scarf at the side seam and at both ends (**H**).

variations

This scarf works best with soft fabrics. It is essential that the tuck-through panel is made from soft fabric that will 'scrunch' easily when the main scarf is tucked through it.

The main body of the scarf also works best in a fine, soft or even stretch velveteen that drapes well when worn. You can introduce colour, texture and pattern at the other end with a piece of fancy silk brocade and a tassel.

E

F

G

H

making **vintage** accessories

beatrice

1920s PLEATED FLAP CLUTCH BAG

Clutch bags, although originally popularized in the 1920s and 30s, have enjoyed something of a revival in recent fashion collections. You could add a narrow fabric or cord handle to the bag to enable it to be slipped over the shoulder, if desired.

The simple envelope shape of the classic clutch bag, which would have been tucked under the arm or held in a gloved hand, lends itself very well to adding decoration or embellishment to the flap, as did the designers of the 1920s.

Variations on embellishments for this bag could include omitting the rose and replacing it with a single large original vintage button and using brocade ribbon or dyed lace to cover the flap seams instead of rickrack. The options are endless.

bag dimensions

Approximately 7in (18cm) tall by 12in (31cm) wide

pattern pieces

A B C D

pages 148–9

suggested fabrics

for main bag fabric:
wool flannel/tweed

for flap trim:
short pile cotton velvet

for bag lining:
patterned silks or cottons

you will need

* 10in (26cm) of main fabric, 54in (140cm) wide

* 10in (26cm) of quilted calico, 54in (140cm) wide as interfacing

* 10in (26cm) of lining fabric, 36in (92cm) wide

* 10in (26cm) x 10in (26cm) of short-pile velvet for flap pleat panel

* 30in (76cm) of jumbo rickrack for flap trim and rose

* 2 pieces x 1½in (4cm) square of craft interfacing (for snap stabilizers)

* 1 magnetic snap set

cutting out

* Cut 2 x piece **A** (front/back) on fold from main fabric

* Cut 2 x piece **A** (front/back) on fold from lining fabric

* Cut 2 x piece **A** (front/back) on fold from interfacing

* Cut 2 x piece **B** (flap front side) from main fabric

* Cut 1 x piece **C** (flap pleat panel) on fold from velvet

* Cut 1 x piece **D** (flap back) on fold from main fabric

* Cut 2 x piece **D** (flap back) on fold from interfacing (iron-on or sew-in)

making up instructions

Step 1
Pin front and back **A** sections to corresponding front and back **A** interfacing sections and baste together. Refer to **Sew-in Interfacing**, page 17.

Step 2
Make the pleats in the velvet flap centre piece **C** by bringing pleat lines together and pressing pleats lightly towards flap centre on the right side (**A**). Stitch a flap side piece to each side of the pleated centre piece, leaving a ½in (13mm) seam (**B**). Press seams open flat.

Step 3
Pin the assembled flap top piece to the flap interfacing piece **D** and baste together round outside edge (**C**). Refer to **Sew-in Interfacing**, page 17. You may need to adjust the fullness of the velvet section slightly to fit and trim any excess fabric from around the interfacing after stitching (**D**). Position jumbo rickrack over seams on both sides of flap, and stitch in place (**E**).

Step 4
Stitch or iron interfacing to wrong side of flap underneath and transfer the magnetic snap position marker. Fix the non-magnetic half of snap. Refer to **How to Apply a Magnetic Snap**, page 18.

Step 5
Pin the two flap pieces right sides together. Stitch together round curved side/lower edges, leaving a ½in (13mm) seam allowance. Trim away any excess, clip into the seam allowance round curves and turn right sides out. Press from reverse, then topstitch all round using a longer stitch length, approx ¼in (6mm) from the edge. Press again.

Step 6
Use one of the interfaced (**A**) sections that you made in Step 1 as your bag front. Transfer the magnetic snap placement marker onto bag front piece and fix magnetic section of snap.

Step 7
Pin the 2 interfaced front/back (**A**) pieces together, right sides of main fabric together. Stitch together around sides and lower edges, leaving a ½in (13mm) seam allowance. Trim the seams back to ⅜in (1cm) to cut down on bulk. Insert your finger into one of the bottom corners. Match up seam on bottom and side, pin through all thicknesses and stitch straight across the corner to form a gusset. Refer to pictures in **Katherine**, pages 54–7, for help with this step. Repeat this on the opposite corner. Turn bag right sides out and press.

Step 8
Pin the finished flap onto the back of the bag, right outside of flap against right outside of bag back, with raw edges even. Baste using a long stitch length, approx ½in (13mm) from the edge.

Step 9

Stitch two lining pieces (A) right sides together at side and lower edges, leaving gap of around 4in (10cm) in the centre of the bottom seam for turning the bag through. Insert your finger into one of the bottom corners. Match up seam on bottom and side, pin through all thicknesses and stitch straight across the corner to form a gusset as you did for the main bag pieces. Repeat this on the opposite corner.

Step 10

Insert bag into lining with right sides together. Pin bag and lining together through all thicknesses round upper edges, having raw edges even. Stitch through all thicknesses using normal stitch length and leaving seam allowance of just over ½in (13mm). Trim seam back to ⅜in (1cm) and clip into the seam allowance at sides.

Step 11

Turn the bag through the opening in the bottom of the lining and push the lining to the inside of the bag.

Refer to **To Line the Bags in this Book**, page 22. Roll the lining with your fingers so that it is not visible from the outside and pin it in place all round top, ensuring that the flap will sit correctly. Topstitch through all layers, about ½in (13mm) from the top of the bag, using a long stitch length.

Step 12

Slip stitch the opening in the lining closed, tuck lining back into bag and give the bag a final press under a cloth. Press first with flap open and then again with flap closed. If necessary, to secure the lining into the bag further, you can hand-stitch a few stitches at the side seams, through bag and lining.

Step 13

Make a rose using jumbo rickrack following instructions in **Clementine**, pages 48–51. Hand-stitch the finished rose to point of the flap (**F**).

Refer to To Line the Bags in this Book, page 22.

Clementine, pages 48–51.

variations

Try making this bag out of patterned fabric or brocade. You could make the main body of the bag from heavy cotton and use a small print cotton fabric for the pleated flap section instead of velvet. Trim the seams with ribbon and finish with a ribbon rose or large button instead of the rickrack.

Fine-weight cotton velvet works well for the pleated section as it has a short pile and gives a sumptuous look without the headaches frequently encountered when sewing and pressing deep-pile velvets. There is only a small panel of velvet, so this is manageable and adds interest and texture without bulk.

beatrice

47

1920s

D

E

F

clementine

1920s RICKRACK JEWELLERY AND TRIMS

In trying to trace the history of rickrack, it appears this durable zigzag woven braid was used as early as the 1880s and remained a favourite among home dressmakers throughout the 20th century.

Rickrack has seen many uses as a flat applied trim or seam insertion, livening up everything from aprons and home accessories to fashion garments. It has enjoyed a revival in recent years with different widths from skinny to jumbo again being sold in haberdashery shops in a rainbow of colours.

I had wondered what else could be done with these charming vintage trims until I purchased an original 1960s pattern that showed how to make rickrack flowers. They were used as flat appliqué, stitched flat to a hat. I developed the idea and came up with some great ways to use these both as trims and as accessories in their own right.

you will need

For the chrysanthemum necklace

✱ 2 small frog fastener sets

✱ Approx 9in (23cm) of twisted cord cut into 2 equal lengths

✱ 1 drop bead approx 1½in (4cm) long and a bead cap to fit

✱ 1 head pin for dangle

✱ 2 eye pins (for 2 connector beads)

✱ 4 antique brass melon beads (4mm size) for connectors and dangle

✱ 5 antique brass jump rings

✱ 4 fold-over box calottes/lace ends

✱ 1 toggle clasp

✱ jewellery pliers

For the rose necklace

✱ 2 small frog fastener sets

✱ Approx 10in (26cm) of (antique tone) chain

✱ 2 head pins

✱ 2 lucite beads (6mm)

✱ 2 metal filligree beads (6mm)

✱ 1 lobster clasp

✱ 1 jump ring

For the chrysanthemum

✱ Approx 18in (46cm) of jumbo rickrack (for outer petals)

✱ Approx 9in (23cm) of medium width rickrack (for inner petals)

✱ 1 vintage glass button for flower centre

For the rose

✱ Approx 24in (61cm) of jumbo rickrack

making up instructions

to make a chrysanthemum

These flowers can be used for numerous trimming purposes and to make stunning textile jewellery.

Step 1

Thread a needle with a long double length of thread to match the jumbo rickrack. Working from the right-hand side of the length of rickrack (or left-hand side if left-handed), thread needle in and out of each of the upper points of the rickrack, along the entire length (**A**).

Step 2

Hold rickrack at one end, pull up gathering thread and make sure the petals are all sitting in the same direction (**B**). Pull up tight and secure the gathering thread with a few stitches.

Step 3

Form the gathered rickrack into a circle, joining the two raw ends of the rickrack together at the back of the flower. Run needle round the inner flower points and pull up thread tight again to secure (**C**).

Step 4

Repeat steps 1 to 3 with the length of medium-width rickrack to form a smaller circle for the centre petals of the flower (**D**).

Step 5

Layer the two circles with the smaller one centred on top. Stitch together at every other petal, through all layers from the back, trying to keep stitches invisible from the front. Stitch vintage button in the centre of the flower (**E**).

to make a double chrysanthemum

The flower on the hat in **Vita**, pages 36–9, was made using a double layer of jumbo rickrack as follows:

Step 1

Cut two pieces of jumbo rickrack in toning colours, each approx 12in (31cm) long. Thread a needle with a long double length of thread to match the rickrack. Lay one length of rickrack on top of the other so that the lower piece is just visible at the top of the upper piece. Working from the right-hand side of the length of rickrack (or the left-hand side if you are left-handed), thread the needle in and out of the upper points of both layers of rickrack at the same time (**F**).

Step 2

Proceed as in steps 2 and 3 above. Then stitch a braid-covered button to the centre of the completed double circle and stitch a tassel to the reverse side of the flower. Finally, stitch a brooch pin to the reverse of the flower near the top edge so that it can be attached to a hat or jacket lapel (**G**).

to make a necklace

I have made necklaces (H)
(with matching bracelets) using
the chrysanthemums and roses as
centrepieces.

Step 1
Make chrysanthemum as detailed
opposite. Stitch two halves of each
frog fastener together so they no
longer come apart. Stitch one
complete frog set each side of the
centre flower at an angle. The frogs
should be stitched to the flower at
the back. Attach them towards the
top of the flower so that the flower
does not 'flip' when being worn.

Step 2
Make the drop and connectors
by threading the relevant beads
onto the eye pins and forming
loops using jewellery pliers. Make
one connector for each side and
then one drop for the front.

Step 3
Attach the dangle to the bottom of
the flower using a jump ring. You
should be able to thread the jump
ring directly through the rickrack at
the back of one of the lower petals.

Step 4
Attach a jump ring to the top of
the frog at each side by threading
through the frog itself. Attach a
connector to the ring at each side.

Step 5
Apply glue at each end of each
piece of the cut twisted cord, then
fold a box calotte over each glued
end. Attach one length of cord to
each connector. Then attach half
of the toggle clasp at each of the
other cord ends using jump rings.

to make a rose

This rose can be used to make
the centrepiece of a necklace as
shown in the picture (I), or if
you make it from narrower rickrack,
it can be used to make a great ring.

Step 1
Fold the length of rickrack in half
and twist it around itself (J) until
you reach the end. Neaten the
ends by tucking them under and
stitching them together so that the
raw edges are not invisible.

Step 2
Starting from the end you have just
neatened, roll the twisted rickrack
length on itself, securing with a few
hand-stitches at the base of the
roll as you go to form a rose (K).
Hand-stitch the end in place.

Step 3
Turn down the petals to form a
rose shape (L).

1930s

katherine

1930s DECO CLUTCH WITH LACE TRIM

This bag design uses the same body as the bag in Beatrice, pages 44–7, but it has a more streamlined look because the flap is asymmetric, which was a very popular look in the early 1930s.

bag dimensions

Approximately 7in (18cm) tall by 12in (31cm) wide

pattern pieces

pages 150–1

suggested fabrics

for main bag:
wool flannel/tweed

for bag lining:
patterned silks

for trim:
tea-dyed cotton lace

Although clutch bags of the 1930s often had jewelled clasps and bakelite frames, this bag is given a splash of detail with a row of lace flowers and heart buttons backed with a strip of wool tweed.

Use patterned vintage fabric, or a strip of ribbon, or use a length of wide lace, omit the lace flowers and use bigger buttons as trim. For a more tailored look, use a leather or suede strip and a large single vintage button trim.

you will need

* 10in (26cm) of main fabric, 54in (140cm) wide

* 10in (26cm) of quilted calico, 54in (140cm) wide as interfacing

* 10in (26cm) of lining fabric, 36in (92cm) wide

* Strip of tweed 8in (20cm) by 2in (5cm), frayed at edges

* Lace with individual flower motifs

* 5 small heart buttons

* 2 pieces x 1½in (4cm) square of craft interfacing (for snap stabilizers)

* 1 magnetic snap set

* fabric glue

cutting out

* Cut 2 x piece **A** (front/back) on fold from main fabric

* Cut 2 x piece **A** (front/back) on fold from lining fabric

* Cut 2 x piece **A** (front/back) on fold from interfacing

* Cut 2 x piece **B** (flap) from main fabric (cut with wrong sides together)

* Cut 1 x piece **B** (flap) from interfacing

* Cut 1 x piece **B** (flap) from iron-on interfacing for underside of flap

making up instructions

Step 1

Pin front and back **A** sections to corresponding front and back **A** interfacing sections and baste together. Refer to **Sew-in Interfacing**, page 17.

Step 2

Make one interfaced **A** section your bag front. Transfer magnetic snap placement marker onto the bag front piece and fix magnetic section of snap in place, referring to **How to Apply a Magnetic Snap**, page 18.

Step 3

Pin the two interfaced front/back **A** pieces together, right sides of main fabric together. Stitch together around sides and lower edges, leaving a ½in (13mm) seam allowance (**A**). Trim the seams back to ⅜in (1cm) to cut down on bulk. Insert your finger into one of the bottom corners. Match up the seam on bottom and side, pin through all thicknesses

(**B**) and stitch straight across the corner to form a gusset. Trim any excess at corner (**C**).

Step 4

Repeat this on the opposite corner. Turn bag right sides out and press.

Step 5

Pin the top half of the flap **B** to corresponding interfacing piece **B** and baste together round outside edge. Refer to **Sew-in Interfacing**, page 17. Fray edges of the tweed strip (**D**). Stitch it to the top flap piece at positions marked on pattern template. Trim excess fabric from strip at top and bottom in line with flap edge (**E**).

Step 6

With fabric glue, position and stick tea-dyed lace flowers down tweed strip (**F**). When glue is dry, stitch a small heart button in the centre of each lace flower.

Step 7

Iron interfacing to wrong side of flap underside and transfer the magnetic snap position marker. Fix the non-magnetic half of snap, referring to **How to Apply a Magnetic Snap**, page 18.

Step 8

Pin the two flap pieces **B** right sides together. Stitch together round curved side/lower edges, leaving a ½in (13mm) seam allowance. Trim away any excess bulk, clip into the seam allowance round curves and turn right sides out. Press from reverse, then topstitch all round using a longer stitch length, approx ½in (13mm) from the edge. Press again.

Step 9

Pin the finished flap onto the back of the bag, right outside of flap against right outside of bag back, with raw edges even. Baste using a long stitch length, approx ½in (13mm) from the edge.

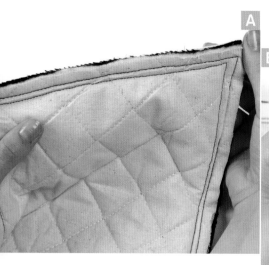

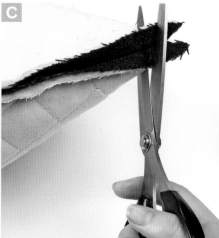

Step 10

With right sides together, stitch lining pieces together at side and lower edges, but leave a gap of around 4in (10cm) in the centre of the bottom seam for turning the bag through. Insert your finger into one of the bottom corners. Match up seam on bottom and side, pin through all thicknesses and stitch straight across the corner to form a gusset as you did for the main bag pieces. Repeat this on the opposite corner.

Step 11

Insert bag into lining with right sides together. Pin bag and lining together through all thicknesses round upper edges, having raw edges even. **NB: You will be pinning through the flap on the back piece, too.** Stitch through all thicknesses using a normal stitch length and leaving seam allowance of just over ½in (13mm). **NB: This will be quite a lot of thicknesses to sew through, so stitch slowly and carefully.** Trim seam back to ⅜in (1cm) and clip into the seam allowance at sides.

For this project I have dyed some white lace using tea to give it an antiqued look. Dyeing lace with tea is simple. Pop a couple of tea bags in a small bowl, pour on boiling water and leave to brew for a couple of minutes. Remove the tea bags, dissolve a couple of teaspoons of salt into the solution and drop the lace into the tea. Leave it for about one hour. The longer you leave it in, the deeper the colour will be: two hours will give a faded tan tone. **NB: this method will only work with cotton or viscose lace and not with synthetics**.

Try making this bag with a co-ordinating pair of tea-dyed lace earrings as in **Diana**, pages 70–3.

Step 12

Turn the bag through the opening in the bottom of the lining and push the lining to the inside of the bag. Refer to **To Line the Bags in this Book**, page 22. Roll the lining with your fingers so that it is not visible from the outside and pin it in place all round the top, ensuring that the flap will sit correctly. Topstitch through all the layers, about ½in (13mm) from the top of the bag, using a long stitch length, and stitching slowly and carefully.

Step 13

Slip stitch the opening in the lining closed, tuck lining back into bag and then give it a final press under a cloth. Press the bag first with flap open and then again with it closed. If necessary, to secure the lining into the bag further, you can hand-stitch a few stitches at the side seams, through bag and lining.

katherine

57

1930s

eleanor

1930s MOTORING CLOCHE WITH ASTRAKHAN TURN-UP

hat dimensions

To fit a medium-size head measurement of approx. 22in (56cm)

pattern pieces

A **B** **C**

pages 152–3

suggested fabrics

for crown:
polar fleece

for front turn-back brim:
fake astrakhan or flat pile fur

for lining:
patterned cotton

I have designed this hat with echoes of the close-fitting motoring cloches of the early 1930s. It is a cheeky style, which, although vintage in its detail, will fit perfectly in place in current fashion accessory wardrobes.

The turn-up brims give the hat more width and the fake astrakhan used at the front of the hat adds texture and interest. Although this style is lined, the whole hat only uses three pattern pieces, the main hat being cut from the same piece in pairs for front and back. I have used polar fleece for the main body of the hat for both comfort and to prevent the panel seams from being too stiff.

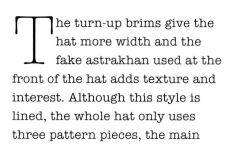

you will need

* 18in (46cm) of polar fleece, 60in (152cm) wide for main hat/brim

* piece of fake astrakhan 7in (18cm) deep by 14in (36cm) wide for front brim

* 11in (28cm) of lining fabric, 36in (92cm) wide

* approx. 24in (61cm) of grosgrain ribbon, 1in (25mm) width for band

cutting out

* Cut 4 x piece **A** (crown) from main fleece (NB: cut 2 pairs with right sides together)

* Cut 4 x piece **A** (crown) from lining fabric (NB: cut 2 pairs with right sides together)

* Cut 2 x piece **B** (back turn-up) on fold from main fabric

* Cut 1 x piece **C** (front turn-up) from fake fur/astrakhan

* Cut 1 x piece **C** (front turn-up) with pattern piece reversed, from fleece

making up instructions

Step 1
Stitch main fleece front sections to back sections **A** at side seams (marked with a broken line on the pattern template), leaving a ½in (13mm) seam allowance (**A**). Press open.

Step 2
Stitch two halves of hat together down centre in one continuous seam (**B**). Turn hat right side out. Mark front seam of hat with a pin to help you identify front and back while you work.

Step 3
Stitch front lining sections **A** to back lining sections **A** at side seams as for hat, leaving a ½in (13mm) seam allowance and press open. Stitch two halves of hat lining together down centre in one continuous seam as for hat.

Step 4
Place lining inside hat, wrong sides together, matching all four seams and having raw edges even (**C**). Stitch together approx ½in (13mm) from the raw edge.

Step 5
Stitch two back turn-up **B** pieces right sides together around upper curved edge, leaving a ½in (13mm) seam allowance. Trim seam back a little to cut down on bulk, clip into seam allowance and turn brim right side out. Press and topstitch about ½in (13mm) from seam. Baste-stitch lower raw edges together.

Step 6
Pin brim to lined hat. Match centre back of turn-up brim to centre back seam of hat. Raw edges should be even and brim should be facing upwards (**D**). Stitch in place approx ½in (13mm) from raw edge.

Step 7
Stitch the astrakhan and fleece sections of front turn-up brim **C** right sides together around edges marked with a dotted line on pattern template, leaving a ½in (13mm) seam allowance. Trim seam allowance back a little to cut down on bulk, clip corner and clip into seam allowance (**E**). Turn brim right side out and press lightly from the fleece side. Baste-stitch raw edges together.

Step 8
Pin front turn-up brim to hat. Match 'x' mark on front brim with centre front seam of hat. Astrakhan should be facing outward, brim pointing upward and raw edges of hat and brim even. **NB: You will be pinning the front brim over the top of the back brim slightly at each side**. Stitch in place approx ½in (13mm) from the raw edge.

*making **vintage** accessories*

Step 9

Zigzag-stitch around the lower raw edges of the hat/brims to prevent any fraying. Try hat on to ascertain sizing. Pin the grosgrain ribbon to the hat covering the seam and zigzagging (refer to **Hats**, pages 24–5, for help with this step). If the hat is a bit large, pin the grosgrain to take in a little of the fullness so that the hat will be tighter.

Step 10

Fold one end of the ribbon over and overlap the two ends of the ribbon with the folded edge on top. Stitch the ribbon in place about ¼in (6mm) from the upper edge of the grosgrain. Hand- or machine-stitch the folded end of the grosgrain ribbon to itself. Turn the ribbon upwards and stitch with a few hand-stitches to the hat lining. For extra neatness and if the hat fits well, as it will be hidden under the turn-up, you could machine-stitch along the top edge of the grosgrain ribbon as

sewing tip

I like the cover button badge because it is both functional in holding the brim in place and decorative. If you make it with a pin back, it could double as a matching lapel ornament.

For this badge, I have stitched a narrow piece of velvet across a circle of toning tweed, and then I have attached a bundle of long chocolate brown feathers to the centre of the circle, and covered it with a tea-dyed lace flower topped with a heart-shaped button to tie in with other projects in the chapter. The feathers hang to one side of the face and I feel they finish the hat off perfectly.

well, right through the lining and hat. Do this with the brim turned down and out of the way (**F**).

Step 11

Turn both brims upwards and pick any fur/astrakhan out of the seams with a blunt needle or bodkin, referring to **Hats**, pages 24–5, if needed (**G**).

Step 12

If desired, make a matching cover button badge, following instructions in **Marianne**, pages 136–9, to pin at the side of the front brim.

eleanor

61

1930s

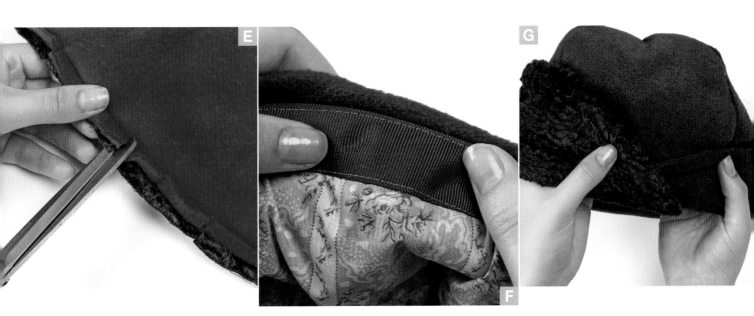

jessica

1930s FLOUNCE SCARF WITH LACE AND RIBBON TRIM

This pretty lightweight scarf with double flounces looks great worn tied at the front with the lace-trimmed end sitting on top. It is not too wide or bulky, giving it a dressier feel than many of the winter scarves found in shops today, the decorative flounces giving a charming feminine vintage appeal.

I have used polar fleece for this project because it offers a great modern alternative to wool. As a 'non-knitter' I tend to use fleece a lot because it offers the warmth and the soft feel of wool without having to do the labour-intensive knitting!

Because polar fleece does not fray, it is not necessary to zigzag the edges to neaten it. The zigzagging serves as a decoration in itself, fluting the edges of the flounces slightly. It also stops the scarf from stretching out of shape.

you will need

✱ 16in (41cm) of polar fleece, 54in (137cm) wide

✱ approx 18in (46cm) of narrow velvet ribbon for trim

✱ 3 lace flowers

✱ 3 vintage buttons

cutting out

✱ Cut 4 x piece (flounce) from polar fleece

✱ Cut 1 rectangle of polar fleece 7½in (19cm) wide by 54in (137cm) long for main scarf

finished scarf dimensions

Approximately 7½in (19cm) wide by 60in (152cm) long

pattern pieces

A

page 154

suggested fabrics

light- to medium-weight polar fleece

making up instructions

Step 1

Position one flounce piece **A** at one end of the main scarf piece, with both pieces right side up and with the flounce edge overlapping the scarf piece by 1in (25mm). Even out the curve of the flounce to fit the straight edge. Pin and stitch in place down centre of overlap (**A**). The stitch line should be ½in (13mm) from the raw edges on both the top and underside of the scarf. Repeat this step with a flounce piece at the other end of the scarf.

Step 2

Trim seam allowances back to ¼in (6mm) on both top and undersides (**B**), then zigzag-stitch along seam allowance, catching in the raw edges of seam on both sides of the scarf. Zigzag-stitch around the entire outside edge of the scarf and attached flounces (**C**).

Step 3

Zigzag-stitch around side and the lower curved edges of both remaining flounce pieces (**D**). Place one of zigzagged flounces at one end of the scarf, positioned 1½in (4cm) above top edge of the first flounce seam. Pull curved edge out so it is straight. Machine-stitch the flounce to the scarf approx. ¼in (6mm) from the upper edge of the flounce (**E**). Repeat step 3 for other end of scarf, then trim back seam allowances.

Step 4

Position and pin a length of velvet ribbon over the upper flounce stitching line, ensuring that the raw edge is covered (**F**). Tuck ends of ribbon under at both ends, then machine-stitch in place down both sides of the ribbon, as close to the edge as possible. Repeat this step at the other end of the scarf.

Step 5

Have fun with the matching trims! At one end of the scarf only, space the lace flowers evenly and centred over the ribbon trim. Place a button at the centre of each flower, then hand-stitch button and flower to scarf at the same time (**G**).

Although I am a polar fleece fan, you could make the scarf from soft wool woven fabric and back it with softly draping velvet. To do this, you would have to add a seam allowance (approx. ½in/13mm) to the outer edges of the main scarf pieces and cut one scarf from wool and a second from lining fabric (velvet or similar).

You would only have one flounce at each end and would have to cut these double (again one from wool and one from velvet) and add a seam allowance at the side and lower edges. Make the flounces first by stitching them right sides together at the side and lower edges, turning them right sides out and stitching the upper raw edges together. Attach a flounce at each end of the scarf, and then stitch the two main scarf pieces together with the flounces sandwiched between them at each end. Remember to leave a gap in the centre to turn the scarf through.

deborah

1930s TRIMMED GLOVES

Although gloves have a long and varied history and were worn throughout the decades in this book, they enjoyed something of a heyday in the 1930s, when an outfit was not considered complete without a pair of gloves.

pattern pieces
A B C

page 154

suggested fabrics

for making cuffs
polar fleece, fake fur or
fake suede

Over the years, fashionable gloves have ranged from long opera style and gauntlet shapes to butter-soft leather and lace trimmed. Today, unless you are the Queen, gloves are largely confined to winter wardrobes or a day at the races.

Gloves can be quite fiddly to make from scratch, but with the fabrics offered today, they are relatively easy to 'customize'.

Polar fleece gloves, for example, although often rather basic, are cheap to buy (particularly in the winter sales) and offer a good basis from which to design your own new and individual pair.

I have concentrated on adding cuffs to gloves, but there are dozens of other techniques and trims you could use to create a great addition to your favourite winter outfit.

you will need

* to make a pair of cuffs for most size gloves, you will need a piece of fleece fabric 22in (56cm) by 6in (15cm)

* leather or felt scraps to co-ordinate for flowers

* small vintage buttons for flower centres

* approx 22in (56cm) rickrack or ribbon trim (per pair of gloves)

cutting out

* Cut 2 x piece **A** (cuff) from fleece

* Cut 2 x flower **B** from felt or leather

* Cut 2 x flower **C** from felt or leather

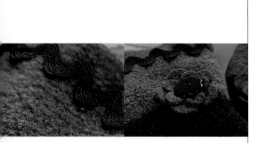

making up instructions

Step 1

Cut approx 2in (5cm) from the top of each purchased fleece glove you wish to customize. The amount you cut from the glove will depend on how long they are and will vary according to different styles. Measure carefully before you cut. As a guide, leave at least 1½in (4cm) – this includes seam allowance – above the top of the glove thumb seam.

Step 2

Cut out cuffs from fleece using template **A**. Stitch a length of rickrack trim about ¾in (2cm) from the upper edge of each cuff (**A**). Note that since you are using polar fleece, it is not necessary to hem the upper edge of the cuff, as fleece does not fray.

Step 3

Machine-stitch the cuff centre back seam with right sides together, leaving a seam allowance of just ¼in (6mm) (**B**).

Step 4

Pin the cuff to the glove, right side of cuff against right side of glove, cuff seam positioned at the centre back of the glove and the wide (top) edge of the cuff facing downwards (**C** and **D**).

Step 5

Stitch cuff to glove leaving a ¼in (6mm) seam allowance. **NB: If you stitch this seam too tight, it will make it harder to get your hand into the glove. Take advantage of the stretch in the fleece**.

Step 6

Using felt or leather, cut out two each of the flowers from templates **B** and **C**. Place each **C** flower on top of each **B** flower and position one double flower on each glove. As the glove is laying flat, the flower centre should be 1in (25mm) away from the outside (little finger) edge of the glove positioned centrally over the seam between cuff and glove.

Step 7

Position one or more small vintage buttons over the flower's centre. Stitching right through the flower, hand-stitch flower and buttons to glove at the same time (**E**).

To make your own cuff template

The pattern template **A** should fit an average sized fleece glove. If you have a wider glove, however, you can easily cut your own cuff pattern template.

Step 1

Measure the width across the glove. Multiply that figure by two and add a ½in (13mm) seam allowance (¼in/6mm for each end) to that figure. On paper, draw a rectangle that figure wide, by the depth you want the cuff to be, plus ¼in (6mm) seam allowance at the upper edge.

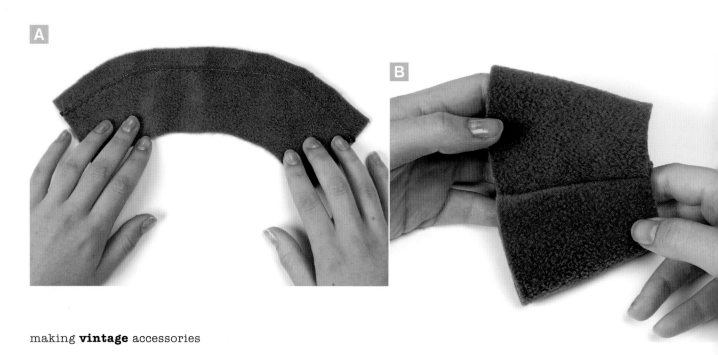

A

B

Step 2

Mark the side seam allowance line at each end of the rectangle and then draw lines from top edge of the rectangle to the lower edge, seven in all, at equal distances along the rectangle. Cut from the top edge to the lower edge *almost* but not entirely to the bottom so that you have seven equal blocks (plus the seam allowance at the end). Lay this cut piece on a bigger piece of paper and fan out the cut sections, allowing the same distance between each block at the top. Pin the blocks to the paper as you go. The wider apart you pull the blocks, the more flared the cuff will be. This is a very good way to experiment with basic pattern cutting.

Redraw round the outside (now curved) edge of the fanned-out piece. This will be your new cuff pattern piece.

The gloves with the fake fur were made using the cuff template **A**. I took a basic pair of grey interlock fabric gloves and cut the top off the gloves as per Step 1 opposite. I then cut two cuffs from fake fur and two from soft wool fabric, but this time I cut a ¼in (6mm) seam allowance at the upper edge of all pieces. I joined the centre back seam in both the fur and wool cuffs, then pinned one wool cuff and one fur cuff right sides together, centre back seams matching. Next, I stitched the wool and fur cuffs together around upper flared edges leaving a ¼in (6mm) seam allowance.

Clip into the seam allowance all round, turn cuffs right (fur) side out and pick the fur out of the upper seam. Next stitch cuff raw edges together round lower edge (now wrong sides

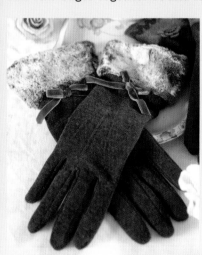

together). Pin and stitch cuff to glove as in Steps 3 and 4 above. Then machine-neaten the seam using a close zigzag stitch. Turn cuff upwards and pick fur out of seam between glove and cuff. Make two bows out of velvet ribbon leaving long tails and stitch one to the centre front of each glove on the seam line.

C

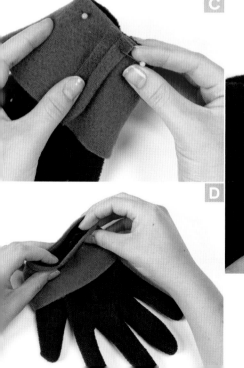

D

E

deborah

69

1930s

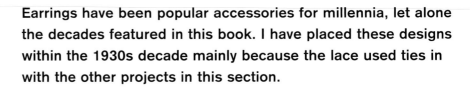

diana

1930s LACE EARRING COLLECTION

Earrings have been popular accessories for millennia, let alone the decades featured in this book. I have placed these designs within the 1930s decade mainly because the lace used ties in with the other projects in this section.

I was inspired to make lace earrings after meeting an artist in Australia who hand-painted lace in exquisite colours. I initially used the lace for use on handbags, but discovered it also makes show-stopping jewellery.

Lace is ideal for earrings as it is lightweight. The trend for chandelier-style earrings translates well into lace because, when stiffened with glue, it is possible to use the weave of the lace in place of metal filigree.

you will need

* ✱ suitable lace with individual elements that can be cut out, preferably cotton or natural fibres if you intend to dye it

* ✱ 1 pair of earring wires

* ✱ jump rings

* ✱ head and eye pins for dangles and connectors

* ✱ a selection of vintage beads, sew-on elements and buttons

* ✱ optional chain for dangles

* ✱ fabric glue

* ✱ jewellery pliers

making up instructions

Step 1

If you are using white or cream lace and wish to 'antique' it, start by dying the lace with tea. Put a couple of tea bags in a small bowl, pour on boiling water and leave to brew for a couple of minutes. Remove the tea bags, dissolve a little salt into the solution and drop the lace into the tea (**A**). Leave it for at least one hour depending on how deep you want the colour to be. One or two hours gives a faded tan tone. Note that this process will only work with cotton or viscose lace and not with synthetics. Rinse thoroughly and dry.

Step 2

Snip apart the individual elements of the lace. Be sure just to cut the connecting threads and not cut into the element itself (**B**).

Step 3

Lay the lace flowers or elements right side facing down onto a piece of waxed kitchen paper. Brush the backs of the lace with fabric glue using a flat brush. This process will not only seal any rough edges and prevent fraying, but will also give body to the lace by stiffening it (**C**). After a few minutes, move the lace a little to make sure it is not stuck to the paper.

Step 4

When the glue is completely dry, stitch any beads or flat stones to the lace centre by hand (**D**).

Step 5

Make any dangles, connectors or drops using the relevant beads, head/eye pins and jewellery pliers. Thread jump rings directly through the lace design at the centre top and bottom of the piece (**E**).

Step 6

Attach dangles and earring wires via the jump rings (**F**).

There are thousands of variations when it comes to making lace earrings.

The **green, gold and black** pair involved stitching a matching vintage button to the centre of the lace, then gluing a black glass vintage flower in the centre of each button. A black bead connector attached to natural brass earring wires finishes the look.

The **antique tan and bronze** pair were made by tea-dying the lace, stitching a vintage pearl at the centre of each lace flower, then attaching an antique cut-glass bead dangle. I have used vintage filigree to attach to the natural brass earring wires.

With the **white daisy** earrings, I simply stiffened the lace with glue. I stitched a flat sew-on cabochon to the centre and made a vintage cut-glass bead dangle using fine silver chain. A smaller vintage bead connector joins the flower to a sterling silver earring wire.

The **blue-green** earrings and the **deep plum** pair were both made using hand-painted lace. I managed to find some beautiful vintage glass tulip beads to tone with the latter and for the blue-green pair I have used Swarovski crystal connector beads in deep blue, attached to the lace via sterling silver jump rings. The clear crystal teardrop elements were stitched to the lace.

1940s

agatha

1940s HANDBAG WITH FANCY POCKET

This handbag is both practical and stylish, offering plenty of room for all the day-to-day essentials. It has both an interior pocket and a fancy pleated pocket on the outside.

I have used wooden handles to complement the cream wool fabric, and tied them in with a pair of decorative vintage buttons. This bag is incredibly versatile: the gusset gives a capacious three-dimensional shape that is relatively easy to assemble and can be adapted with different trims or handles.

bag dimensions

Approximately 14in (36cm) wide by 9in (23cm) tall (excluding handle) Gusset depth 3in (8cm)

pattern pieces

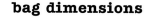

pages 155–7

suggested fabrics

for main bag fabric:
plain wool flannel/tweed

for bag lining:
silk jacquard or fancy cotton print

you will need

* 18in (46cm) of main fabric, 60in (152cm) wide

* 18in (46cm) of lining fabric, 60in (150cm) wide

* 18in (46cm) of quilted calico as interfacing, 36in (92cm) wide

* piece of iron-on interfacing for handle carriers and pocket top – approx 5in (13cm) by 30in (76cm)

* 2 wooden handles with screw-in bars approx 7½in (19cm) wide by 3in (8cm) deep

* 2 large vintage buttons to match

* 2 pieces x 1½in (4cm) square of craft interfacing (for snap stabilizers)

* 1 magnetic snap set

cutting out

* Cut 3 x piece **A** (top front, and front/back facing) on fold from main fabric

* Cut 1 x piece **B** (lower front and lining front/back) on fold from main fabric

* Cut 3 x piece **B** (lower front and lining front/back) on fold from lining, for lining and internal pocket

* Cut 1 x piece **C** (gusset) on fold from main fabric

* Cut 1 x piece **C** (gusset) on fold from interfacing

* Cut 1 x piece **C** (gusset) on fold from lining

* Cut 1 x piece **D** (pocket) from main fabric

* Cut 1 x piece **E** (back and interfacing front/back) on fold from main fabric for back

* Cut 2 x piece **E** (back and interfacing front/back) on fold from interfacing

* Cut 1 x piece **F** (pocket lining) from lining fabric (cut on wrong side of fabric)

* Cut 2 x handle carrier piece (to fit your handle) from main fabric

* Cut 2 x handle carrier piece (to fit your handle) from iron-on interfacing

making up instructions

Step 1

Make pleats in pocket piece **D** by bringing pleat lines together. Pin in place first, then press with pleats facing towards the left on the outside of the pocket (**A**). Iron a piece of interfacing to wrong side of pocket-lining piece along top scalloped edge. This will help stabilize the top edge of the pocket. Trim interfacing to fit. (Remember to cut the lining piece on the wrong side of the lining fabric.) Then stitch pocket piece to pocket lining **F** right sides together along edge marked with broken line on pocket-lining piece. Clip into seam allowance around curves (**B**) and turn pocket right side out (**C**).

Step 2

Press pocket and topstitch along edge marked with broken line on pocket-lining piece, approx ½in (13mm) from edge. Pin and stitch lined pocket to bag lower front **B** along pleated raw edge, outside edges, and then topstitch the pocket to bag lower front from dot along seamed pocket edge marked with broken line on pocket piece (**D**). You may need to adjust the fullness in the pocket to fit. All edges should be aligned.

Step 3

With right sides together, pin and stitch bag lower front (now with pocket attached) to upper front piece **A** (**E**), using a seam of ½in (13mm). Press seam towards top and topstitch approx ½in (13mm) from seam.

Step 4

Pin assembled bag front to corresponding front interfacing section **E** and baste together round entire outside edge. Refer to **Sew-in Interfacing**, page 17. Using a solid interfacing such as quilted calico and adjusting the assembled front to fit the interfacing ensures that the bag front will be the same size and shape as the back.

Step 5

Pin bag back **E** and bag gusset pieces **C** to the corresponding interfacing pieces and then baste together, referring to **Sew-in Interfacing**, page 17. Pin bag front to bag gusset matching dots. Stitch together along lower edge between the dots. Stitch bag back to gusset in the same way between dots. Then pin and stitch the bag together at sides from the top edge to the dots (see **Lauren**, pages 80–3, for pictures of this step). Clip into the seam allowance at the curved edges. Turn bag right side out and press.

Step 6

Make handle carriers to fit your handles, referring to **Handle Carriers**, page 21, throughout this step. If you are using screw-in handles, attach only the carriers to the bag, but if using solid or ring handles, attach handles via carriers to the bag at this point.

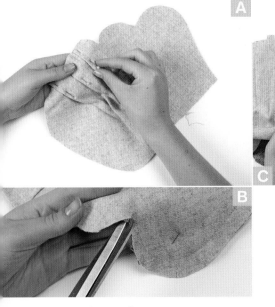

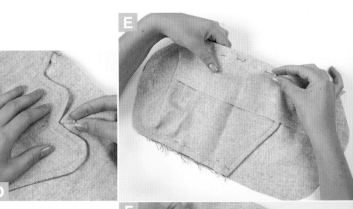

Pin the handle carriers on outside of bag, positioned at centre front and centre back with raw edges even. Machine-baste in place.

Step 7
If you are making an internal pocket, make this next. Hem upper edge of one lining piece **B** with a narrow hem. Stitch front/back lining pieces to front/back facing pieces using a ½in (13mm) seam allowance. Press seams toward bottom and topstitch if desired. Lay the pocket piece on to one of the assembled front/back lining/facing pieces. Stitch from pocket marker on one side, along top, around lower raw edge and to pocket marker on other side. This should leave a pocket opening of approx 6in (15cm) in the centre (**F**).

Step 8
Transfer the magnetic snap position markers onto the facing/lining pieces and fix magnetic snap to both sides opposite each other. Refer to **How to Apply a Magnetic Snap**, page 18.

Step 9
Pin bag front lining **B** to bag gusset lining **C** matching dots. Stitch together along lower edge between the dots as for main bag.

Leave a gap of about 4in (10cm) in the centre of this seam to enable you to turn the bag. **NB: If you are using solid handles, make sure you leave a gap big enough for the handles to fit through.** Stitch bag back lining **B** to gusset between dots. Then stitch bag lining together at sides from the top edge to the dots.

Step 10
Insert the bag into lining with right sides together. Pin bag and lining together through all thicknesses round the upper edges, having raw edges even. **NB: You will be pinning through the handle carriers.** Stitch through all thicknesses using a normal stitch length and leaving a seam allowance of just over ½in (13mm). Trim seam back to ⅜in (1cm) and clip into seam allowance at sides.

Step 11
Turn the bag right side out through the opening in the bottom of the lining and push the lining to the inside of the bag. Refer to **To Line the Bags in this Book**, page 22. Roll the facing with your fingers so that it is not visible from the outside and pin it in place all round top. Topstitch through all layers, about ½in (13mm) from the top of the bag, using a long stitch length.

Step 12
Slipstitch the opening in the lining closed, tuck lining back into bag and give the bag a final press under a cloth. If necessary, to secure the lining into the bag

variations

You can always make this bag with the long fabric handle from **Lauren**, pages 80–3, instead of using wooden handles if you would prefer a shoulder bag. If you are not confident enough to tackle the front fancy pocket, for a more simple option you could omit the pocket and use a flat or 3D appliqué on the front instead.

This bag uses a facing because there is no flap. If you prefer, you can line all the way to the top, especially if you have a pretty co-ordinating lining that you would like to reveal. Simply cut the front/back lining pieces from piece **E** (back and front/back interfacing) instead and omit the facings.

further, you can hand-stitch a few stitches at the side seams, through bag and lining.

Step 13
Hand-stitch two vintage buttons in place on front pocket (**G**).

lauren

1940s UTILITY FLAP SHOULDER BAG

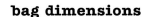

This bag was inspired by my favourite era for accessories, the inventive wartime years – and its practical shape and size gives more room for the contents of a modern-day woman's handbag!

During the Second World War, interest was often added to a bag design by the use of an unusually shaped flap. It offers a great way to use a piece of fancy fabric – in this case a piece of precious tweed I rescued from an old jacket – to offset the plainness off the utilitarian weave. The velvet in the pleated panel and handle give texture and a hint of luxury.

bag dimensions

Approximately 14in (36cm) wide by 9in (23cm) tall (excluding handle); gusset depth 3in (8cm); handle 22in (56cm) long

pattern pieces

Ⓐ Ⓑ Ⓒ Ⓓ Ⓔ Ⓕ Ⓖ

page 158–161

suggested fabrics

for main bag:
wool flannel/tweed

for bag flap:
fancy patterned tweed

for pleated front panel:
short-pile cotton velvet

for lining:
firm-weight silk or dress cotton

you will need

✱ 18in (46cm) of main fabric, 36in (92cm) wide for top front/sides, back and base

✱ 14in (36cm) of velvet, 30in (76cm) wide for pleat panel and handle

✱ 20in (51cm) by 8in (20cm) of fancy tweed for flap

✱ 11in (28cm) by 28in (71cm) of iron-on interfacing for handle and flap

✱ 20in (51cm) of lining fabric, 36in (92cm) wide for lining

✱ 20in (51cm) of quilted calico, 36in (92cm) wide for interfacing

✱ 1 cover button approx 2in (5cm) diameter

✱ 2 pieces x 1½in (4cm) square of craft interfacing (for snap stabilizers)

✱ 1 magnetic snap set

cutting out

✱ Cut 1 x piece Ⓐ (top front) on fold from main fabric

✱ Cut 2 x piece Ⓑ (lower front side) from main fabric

✱ Cut 1 x piece Ⓒ (back) on fold from main fabric

✱ Cut 2 x piece Ⓒ (front/back lining) on fold from interfacing

✱ Cut 2 x piece Ⓒ (front/back lining) on fold from lining fabric

✱ Cut 1 x piece Ⓓ (front pleated panel) on fold from velvet

✱ Cut 1 x piece Ⓔ (gusset) on fold from main fabric

✱ Cut 1 x piece Ⓔ (gusset) on fold from interfacing

✱ Cut 1 x piece Ⓔ (gusset) on fold from lining fabric

✱ Cut 2 x piece Ⓕ (flap) on fold from fancy tweed

✱ Cut 2 x piece Ⓕ (flap) on fold from iron-on interfacing

✱ Cut 1 x piece Ⓖ (handle) on fold from velvet

✱ Cut 1 x piece Ⓖ (handle) on fold from iron-on interfacing

making up instructions

Step 1
Make pleats in centre front pleated panel **D** by bringing together pleat lines and pressing pleats lightly towards outside edges of panel on both sides, from reverse (**A**). Stitch pleats in place along top edge of panel (with folded edge of pleats facing centre on wrong side). Stitch front sides **B** to centre front pleated panel, leaving ½in (13mm) seam allowance (**B**). Press seams toward centre.

Step 2
Stitch assembled front centre and sides to top front piece **A**, leaving ½in (13mm) seam allowance (**C**). Press seam towards top and topstitch ¼in (6mm) from the seam.

Step 3
Pin assembled bag front to corresponding front interfacing section **C** and baste together

round entire outside edge. Refer to **Sew-in Interfacing**, page 17. Make sure that the lower curved edge of the pleated velvet panel aligns with the straight lower edge of the interfacing. Using a solid interfacing such as quilted calico and adjusting the assembled front to fit the interfacing ensures that the bag front will stay the same size and shape as the back.

Step 4
Transfer the magnetic snap position marker onto the outside of the bag front and fix magnetic half of snap. Refer to **How to Apply a Magnetic Snap**, page 18.

Step 5
Pin bag back **C** and bag gusset pieces **E** to the corresponding interfacing pieces and then baste together, referring to **Sew-in Interfacing**, page 17. Pin bag front to bag gusset matching dots.

Stitch together along lower edge between the dots (**D**). Stitch bag back to gusset in the same way between dots (**E**). Pin and stitch bag together at sides from the top edge to the dots (**F**). Clip into seam allowance at curved edges. Turn bag right side out and press.

Step 6
Iron interfacing to wrong side of both flap pieces **F**. Transfer the magnetic snap position marker onto the underside piece of the flap and fix non-magnetic half of snap. Refer to **How to Apply a Magnetic Snap**, page 18.

Step 7
Pin both flap sections right sides together. Stitch together round sides/lower edges, leaving ½in (13mm) seam allowance. Trim excess bulk, clip into seam allowance at corners and lower curves and turn right sides out.

Press flat, then topstitch all round using a longer stitch length, ½in (13mm) from edge. Press again.

Step 8

Pin the finished flap to the back of the bag centrally, right outside of flap against right outside of bag back, having raw edges even. Baste using a long stitch length, approx. ½in (13mm) from the edge.

Step 9

Make handle. Iron interfacing onto reverse side of handle piece 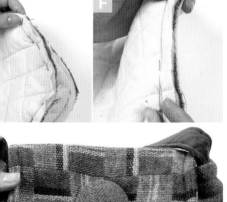 and fold in long raw edges to centre. Fold handle in half lengthways and topstitch together down open side and again along closed side, approx. ¼in (6mm) from edges. Refer to **Self-fabric Handles**, page 20.

Step 10

On outside, position centred over side seams with raw edges even, pin handle to bag and baste in place. Refer to **Attaching Long Handles to Bags**, page 20.

Step 11

Pin bag front lining **C** to bag gusset lining **E** matching dots. Stitch together along lower edge between the dots as for main bag. Leave a gap of about 4in (10cm) in one of the centre bottom seams to enable you to turn the bag right way out. Stitch back lining **C** to gusset lining between dots. Then stitch bag lining together at sides from the top edge to the dots as for main bag.

Step 12

Insert the bag into lining with right sides together. Pin bag and lining together through all thicknesses round upper edges, having raw edges even. **NB: You will be pinning through the flap and the handle, too.** Stitch through all thicknesses using a normal stitch length and leaving a seam allowance of just over ½in (13mm). Trim seam back to ⅜in (1cm) and clip into the seam allowance at the sides.

Step 13

Turn bag right side out through the opening in the bottom of the lining and push the lining to the inside of the bag. Refer to **To Line the Bags in this Book**, page 22. Roll the lining with your fingers so that it is not visible from the outside and pin it in place all round top, ensuring that the flap will sit correctly. Topstitch through all layers, about ½in (13mm) from the top of the bag, using a long stitch length.

Step 14

Slip stitch the opening in the lining closed, tuck lining back into bag and give bag a final press under a cloth. Press first with flap open and then again with flap closed. If necessary, to secure the lining into the bag further, you can hand-stitch a few stitches at the side seams, through bag and lining.

Step 15

Cover a large button with the main fabric and hand-stitch it to the flap (**G**).

83

If you do not want to make the pleated panel, you could simply cut two back **C** pieces instead and use one for your front. Still make the flap in a contrasting fabric to keep some detail. If you choose to use all of the pattern pieces, you will find it is ideal for piecing contrasting quilting fabrics together. There are lots of ways you can combine patterned and plain fabrics to create different looks.

annie

1940s TURBAN STYLE HAT WITH RUCHING

hat dimensions

To fit a medium-size head measurement of approx. 22in (56cm)

pattern pieces

pages 162–3

suggested fabrics

medium-weight polar fleece and soft cotton velvet

Turban styles were popularized in the war years. I have designed this inventive hat based on just two main pattern pieces – the hat gains all of its shape from careful gathers, ruches and tucks. Although it looks complicated, it is actually quite straightforward to make, looks great on and is well worth the time.

I have used polar fleece in this design, for ease of wear and because the softness is essential to the detailing.

However, I have made half of the hat in toning soft cotton velvet in order to add texture, interest and a period feel.

you will need

* 18in (46cm) of polar fleece, 45in (114cm) wide
* 18in (46cm) of soft cotton velvet, 18in (46cm) wide
* 8in (20cm) of 12mm-width cotton tape
* 16in (41cm) of 6mm-width cotton tape
* 1 cover button approx 2in (5cm) diameter
* large blunt needle or bodkin

cutting out

* Cut 2 x piece **A** (front/back) from fleece, right sides together
* Cut 2 x piece **A** (front/back) from velvet, right sides together
* Cut 1 x piece **B** (band) on fold from fleece

making up instructions

Step 1

Stitch the 12mm-wide cotton tape down the centre front of the hatband **B**. Stitch close to both sides of the tape. This tape will act as a casing for you to thread the 6mm-wide tape through.

Step 2

Thread the narrow tape through a big blunt needle or bodkin and thread through the wide tape casing (**A**). When the end of the narrow tape is almost level with the top of the casing, machine-stitch across a couple of times to secure the narrow tape at the top.

Step 3

Pull up the narrow tape to ruche the front of the hatband to a width of about 3in (8cm) (**B**), then stitch across the other end of the narrow tape to secure it and the ruches in place. Trim the excess narrow tape at both ends.

Step 4

Stitch the centre back seam in the hatband, leaving approx ¾in (2cm) seam allowance. **NB: You may wish to try the headband for sizing, making the seam bigger or smaller**. Press open and topstitch seam allowance in place either side of seam line. Fold the band in half *wrong* sides together so that raw edges are even and pin in place (**C**). Sew raw edges together all round band, approx. ½in (13mm) from the raw edge.

Step 5

As this hat is unlined, it pays to neaten the edges of the velvet pieces before you start, either with a machine zigzag stitch or an overlocker. With right sides together, stitch one velvet front/back piece **A** to another fleece front/back piece **A** leaving a ½in (13mm) seam allowance. Press seam open (**D**). Repeat with the remaining front/back velvet and fleece sections **A**.

Step 6

Stitch hat front and back together in one continuous seam from one side of the hat to the other (**E**). Turn hat right side out. **NB: When you are looking at the hat face on, half of the hat should be velvet and the other half should be fleece**. (The velvet pieces will be stitched to each other at one side seam and the fleece pieces will be stitched to each other at the other side seam.)

Step 7

Pin band to hat, with outside of band against right side of hat and keeping raw edges even. Have ruche line matching hat centre front seam and band centre back seam matching hat centre back seam. Stitch in place, leaving a ½in (13mm) seam allowance. Neaten seam allowance by zigzagging or overlocking edges together.

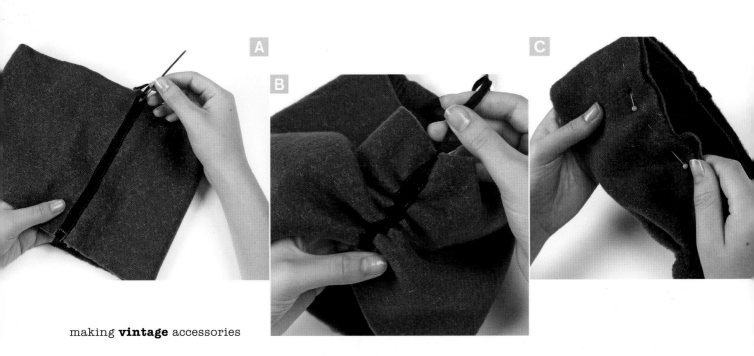

Step 8

Thread a needle with a double thickness of strong thread. Make a knot at the end and secure in place from wrong side of hat at 'x' mark, at base of gathering line marked on pattern template at the top of the hat. In the ditch of the centre seam, run a gathering straight stitch up the seam, over the top of hat and back down the seam the other side to the 'x' marker on the back of the hat. Pull up the gathers to approx. 3in (8cm) on each side of the hat. Secure the thread on the inside (**F**). **NB: This part of the hat will not get any pull on it – the gathering is purely decorative**.

Step 9

At both side seams and at the centre back seam, just above the hat band, tuck the hat downwards to make tucks that are in 2in (5cm) deep. Secure the tucks by machine-stitching in the ditch of the seams for 1in (25mm) from the top of each tuck (**G**).

variations

When you wear the hat, ensure that it is tucked down properly at the sides and back. You can play around with it to make it sit differently on the head and give a variety of looks. I quite like the top gathered section to sit facing back a little. If you would prefer the top of the hat to stand up more, you can also stitch a tuck at centre front seam.

I have made this hat for myself in black and it has become a wardrobe staple. People always comment on how different it looks. You could even try making it with half of the hat in patterned fleece, soft tweed or printed velvet for a more marked contrast.

Step 10

Cover the button with velvet and stitch in place centred over the tuck at the velvet side of the hat.

celia

1940s ASYMMETRIC FUR SCARF COLLAR

I have based the design of this scarf collar, or 'tippet', on the asymmetric styles of the late 1930s and early 40s. In those years, collars, stoles and scarves would have been made from real fur, but today there are lots of modern synthetic versions that look fantastic and wear even better than the real thing.

A N outfit in this period would usually have been given the finishing touches with a hat, a matching scarf, cravat or tippet, and often a pair of toning gloves. A fur tippet is still a simple and effective way to add a touch of classic vintage glamour to a modern outfit.

you will need

* 12in (31cm) of fake fur, 36in (92cm) wide for collar
* 12in (31cm) of wool flannel or similar, 36in (92cm) wide for lining/backing
* 2 vintage buttons for trim
* 2 large snap fasteners

cutting out

* Enlarge copy and join pattern template pieces **A** and **B** matching 'o' and 'x' symbols as directed to form one pattern piece. The two edges should be placed and joined side by side and not overlapped.

* Then cut 1 complete collar out of fake fur fabric

* Cut 1 complete collar with pattern piece **reversed** from lining fabric **NB: Remember to mark the upper edge of the collar with pins so that you can identify which way up the collar should go as you are working.**

collar dimensions

Approximately 31in (79cm) long

pattern pieces

pages 164–5

suggested fabrics

for collar:
fake fur

for backing:
soft wool flannel

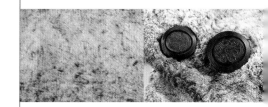

making up instructions

Step 1
With right sides together, pin fur section of collar to the collar backing section. Pin all round with pins at right angles to the raw edge. If you sew carefully, then you can leave the pins in while you stitch to help prevent the fur from 'walking' as you sew.

Step 2
Stitch round entire outside edge of collar from lower back, leaving a ½in (13mm) seam allowance (**A**). Remember to leave a gap at the lower centre back of about 1½in (4cm) to turn the collar through (**B**).

Step 3
Clip into the seam allowance round curved edges and clip corners. Turn the collar right side out through the gap you left at the back. Poke corners using the blunt end of a pencil and smooth curves with your fingers through the gap before slipstitching the gap closed (**C**).

Step 4
Pick the fur out of the seam all round using a blunt needle or bodkin. You may wish to press the collar very lightly from the back, but try to avoid squashing the pile on the fur.

Step 5
Transfer snap marker positions from pattern template and stitch one half of each of the snaps to collar's fur side. Position and stitch other halves of snaps to collar's wool underside so collar fastens and sits comfortably (**D**).

NB: I have not marked on the pattern template where the underside of snaps should go. This is so that you can try the collar on and ascertain where to stitch the snaps based on comfort and fit.

Step 6
Stitch the buttons to the outside of the fur collar at positions marked on pattern template (**E**).

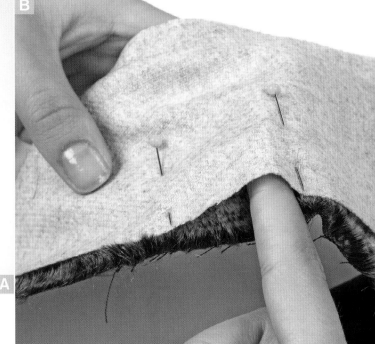

This collar works equally well made up in fleece fabric, triple- stitched around the outside edges and finished with fleece leaves or a corsage. If you are a dressmaker, next time you make a jacket or top, try making a collar in the same fabric as your garment. It makes a great finishing touch and the bonus is that it is a detachable optional extra.

You could make a pair of fur-trimmed gloves to match the collar as in **Deborah**, pages 66–9. Another option for a smart ensemble would be to make the bag in **Lauren**, pages 80–3, with a fake-fur flap to match this collar, instead of using fancy tweed.

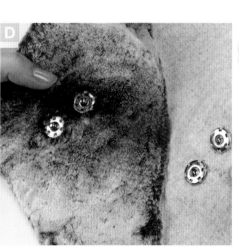

ivy

1940s VINTAGE BUCKLE JEWELLERY

necklace dimensions

finished necklace
16in (41cm) long

Ever since I was left an old tin of vintage buckles by a family friend who was a dressmaker during the 1940s and 50s, I have been fascinated with the inventive shapes, colours and details found in these forgotten haberdashery items. I often looked at these Bakelite treasures originally destined to become belt fastenings, and thought they would make wonderful jewellery.

Several years down the track, I decided that stacking a collection of vintage elements together could create wonderfully unique brooches, while drilling the tops of the buckles could transform them into stunning pendants.

The ideas in this project are simple, and rely largely upon having a good eye for matching colour and shape. Because all of the buckles, buttons and beads you will come across are different, I have outlined some examples of what is possible.

you will need

To make vintage buckle brooches

* ✻ a selection of vintage buckles in different sizes (Bakelite, Lucite, shell or modern plastic)

* ✻ a selection of vintage buttons or cabochons (Bakelite, Lucite, shell or modern plastic)

* ✻ brooch pins (ones with bars or flat pads, depending on the shape of the buckle you are using)

* ✻ glue (see tip box)

To make a vintage buckle necklace

* ✻ 1 black vintage (plastic) buckle

* ✻ 1 small round mother-of-pearl buckle

* ✻ 1 black vintage (plastic) button

* ✻ 3 small flower-shaped mother-of-pearl buttons

* ✻ 1 black tassel, approx 3in (8cm) long

* ✻ 1 jump ring

* ✻ 1 black frog fastener

* ✻ 32in (82cm) of rat-tail satin cord (cut into two 16in/41cm lengths)

* ✻ glue (see tip box)

making up instructions

to make vintage buckle brooches

Step 1
Collect your individual brooch elements – buckles, buttons, cabochons, brooch pin and glue – and assemble them on a piece of waxed paper to protect your work surface (**A**). You can apply most types of glue straight from the tube, but have a small brush and some kitchen paper ready to wipe off spills and mistakes while the glue is still wet.

Step 2
Working on a flat surface, stack the individual elements for the brooch, with the largest at the bottom (**B**). When you are happy with the arrangement, glue the elements together. **NB: Make sure that there is good surface contact between the elements. Try to use buttons that are not domed and buckles that have a flat area or wide bar to which the other elements can be glued securely**.

It also pays to 'rough up' the surface of both the pin and of the buckle/button with a needle file in order to give the glue a better grip. Take care not to damage the buckle, though.

Step 3
Leave the brooch to dry face up. When glue on the brooch has dried completely (**C**), glue a brooch bar to the back of the piece, nearer the top of the buckle so that it will not hang down when being worn (**D**). If you have a domed element at the front, you will have to make sure you have somewhere to leave the pieces to dry so that they are propped up sitting flat, ensuring that the pins will not slide off the back as the glue is setting.

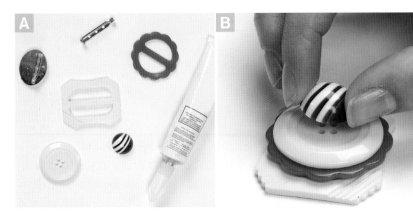

to make a vintage buckle necklace

Step 1
If you are making a pendant from your buckle, you should drill a hole centrally at the top of the buckle, *before* you glue any other elements to it. I have used a standard electric drill on a slow setting (so that it doesn't melt the plastic) using the smallest drill bit I could find. Put the buckle in a vice with padding either side, and screw the vice together slowly to avoid damaging or breaking the buckle. Be careful to ensure that the drill does not slip and make a few practice holes on a scrap button first until you get the technique right. For the black pendant shown in the picture, I have also drilled a hole at the bottom of the buckle through which to attach the tassel.

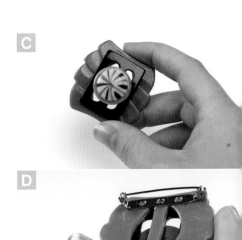

sewing tip

Never throw away odd buttons, buckles or beads. Start collecting a stash of components ready to make buckle brooches and pendants to match all of your outfits. You could also use the brooches as removable trims for the bags in this book.

sewing tip

Finding the right glue is essential to this project. I have found the best option is E6000 Industrial Strength Multi-purpose Adhesive which is available in small tubes. Although it smells slightly when you first use it (this will eventually wear off as the glue dries up), it is the strongest and most effective I have found. Other options for jewellery making are 527 Multi-purpose Cement or a two-part epoxy resin suitable for use with metal and plastics.

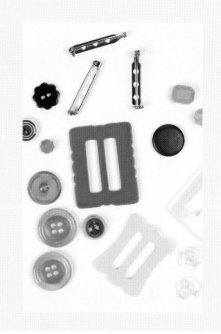

Step 2

Glue the other elements to the buckle as detailed in Steps 2 and 3 for the brooch (excluding the pin) and leave to dry. Attach a jump ring through the hole at the top of the buckle pendant. Attach the tassel to the bottom of the pendant. I cut the loop at the top of the tassel carefully, then threaded it through the hole at the bottom of the buckle pendant, retied the tassel loop at the back near the top of the tassel, then worked the loop ends into the tassel with a needle.

Step 3

Cut the rat-tail cord into two equal lengths, then stitch and bind the two pieces together at one end using matching thread. Stitch the joined cord to one half of the frog fastener at the back (**E**).

Step 4

Stitch and bind the other ends of the cord together, thread the pendant onto the double cord via the jump ring, then stitch the other half of the frog fastener to the remaining cord end. Stitch a flower-shaped button to the top side of the frog fastener on both sides (**F**). The finished necklace does up via the frog fastener (**G**).

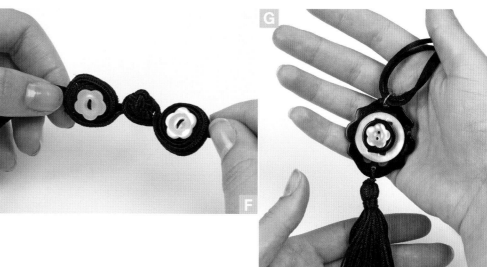

making **vintage** accessories

1950s

connie

1950s ROUNDED TIE-FASTENING HANDBAG

This bag is an elegant but practical design, ideal for use with patterned fabrics. It has an oval base onto which the bag is pleated to give it a three-dimensional stand alone shape.
The wide handle is curved at the base so that it, too, stands up.

I have chosen to finish the bag with co-ordinating velvet ribbon ties, but it would work equally well with a button and loop, or frog closure.

This beautiful spotted Welsh wool tweed in muted powdery blue shades evokes the patterns of the 1950s, providing the perfect fancy accompaniment to the plainer-toned hat of **Iris**, pages 102–5, and the collar, **Molly**, pages 106–9, both of which are in this chapter.

bag dimensions

Approximately 9in (23cm) tall (excluding handle) by 13in (33cm) wide; handle 15½in (39cm) long

pattern pieces

A **B** **C**

page 166–7

suggested fabrics

for main bag fabric:
spotty wool tweed

for lining:
firm weight silk or cotton

you will need

* 18in (46cm) of wool tweed, minimum of 45in (114cm) wide for main bag
* 13in (33cm) of quilted calico, 45in (114cm) wide for interfacing
* 13in (33cm) of lining fabric, 45in (114cm) wide for lining
* 18in (46cm) x 10in (26cm) of iron-on interfacing for handle
* 36in (92cm) of velvet ribbon, ⅝in (16mm) wide, cut in two

cutting out

* Cut 2 x piece **A** (front/back) on fold from main fabric
* Cut 2 x piece **A** (front/back) on fold from interfacing
* Cut 2 x piece **A** (front/back) on fold from lining fabric
* Cut 1 x piece **B** (base) from main fabric
* Cut 1 x piece **B** (base) from interfacing
* Cut 1 x piece **B** (base) from lining fabric
* Cut 2 x piece **C** (handle) on fold from main fabric
* Cut 2 x piece **C** (handle) on fold from iron-on interfacing

making up instructions

NB: The step-by-step pictures show plain tweed being used so that the pleat details are more clearly visible.

Step 1

Pin the bag front/back **A** to the corresponding front/back interfacing sections **A** and baste together (**A**). Refer to **Sew-in Interfacing**, page 17. Make pleats at lower edge on either side of front/back pieces by bringing pleat lines together and pushing pleat toward bag centre on the *wrong* side. Pin in place with pleats facing outwards on the outside (**B**) then stitch in place making sure raw edges are aligned (**C**).

Step 2

With right sides together, stitch front and back sections together down side seams using a ½in (13mm) seam allowance (**D**). Clip into seam allowance at curves.

Step 3

Pin bag base **B** to corresponding base interfacing piece **B** and baste together, referring to **Sew-in Interfacing**, page 17. Pin bag base to bag front/back at lower pleated edge. Match 'x' marks with side seams (**E**). Stitch together, leaving a ½in (13mm) seam allowance. Clip into the seam allowance around curved edges. Turn bag right side out (**F**).

Step 4

Make the handle. Iron interfacing to wrong side of both handle pieces **C**. Stitch handle pieces right sides together down, both long edges approx. ¼in (6mm) from raw edge. Clip into seam allowance and turn handle right side out. Press and topstitch approx ¼in (6mm) from edge (**G**).

Step 5

Pin and stitch handle to the bag, centering over the side seams with the raw edges of the bag and handle even (**H**).

Step 6

Cut ribbon length in half and stitch a piece to centre front/back opposite each other with raw edge of ribbon even with upper raw edge of bag. Cut other ribbon ends at an angle to prevent fraying.

Step 7

Make pleats at lower edge on either side of front/back lining pieces **A** as for main bag. Pin in place, then stitch in place making sure raw edges are aligned.

Step 8

With right sides together, stitch front and back lining together down side seams using a ½in (13mm) seam allowance.

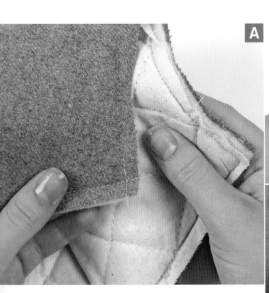

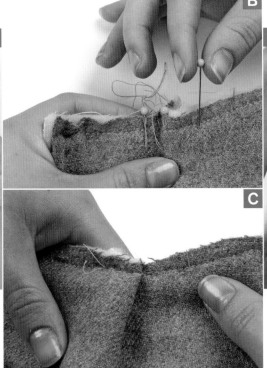

Step 9

Pin lining base **B** to lining front/back at lower pleated edge. Match 'x' marks with side seams as for main bag. Stitch using a ½in (13mm) seam allowance but leave a 4in (10cm) gap at one side through which to turn the bag.

Step 10

Insert bag into lining with right sides together. Pin bag and lining together through all thicknesses round upper edges, keeping raw edges even. **NB: You will be pinning through the handle and ribbons, too**. Stitch through all thicknesses using a normal stitch length and leaving a seam allowance of just over ½in (13mm). **NB: This will be quite a lot of thicknesses to sew through, so stitch slowly and carefully**. Trim seam back to ⅜in (1cm) and clip into the seam allowance at curved points and sides.

Step 11

Turn the bag through the opening in the bottom of the lining and push the lining to the inside of the bag. Refer to **To Line the Bags in this Book**, page 22. Roll the lining with your fingers so that it is not visible from the outside and pin it in place around the top. Topstitch through all layers, about ½in (13mm) from the top of the bag, using a long stitch length.

Step 12

Slip stitch the opening in the lining closed, tuck lining back into bag and give the bag a final press under a cloth. If necessary, to secure the lining into the bag further, you can hand-stitch a few stitches at the side seams, through bag and lining.

Step 13

Tie ribbons in a bow (**I**).

connie

101

1950s

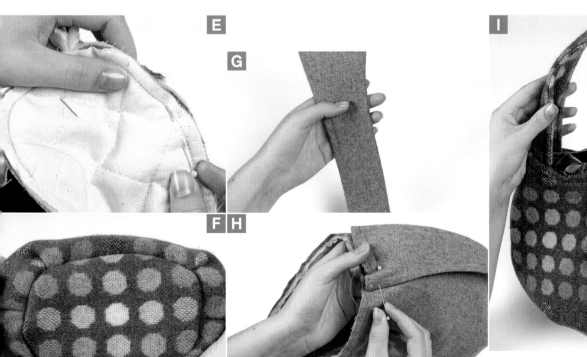

making **vintage** accessories

iris

1950s TUCK HAT WITH BOW TRIM

This cute unlined hat has period detailing but retains a modern look. I developed the main pieces for the hat based on an original 1950s style that would probably have been stiffened with traditional millinery materials.

hat dimensions

To fit a medium-size head measurement of approx. 22in (56cm)

pattern pieces

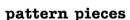

Ⓐ Ⓑ Ⓒ Ⓓ Ⓔ

pages 168–70

suggested fabrics

polar fleece

Although this design looks quite complicated, it uses just three main pattern pieces. The tuck gives the design a tailored look even though it is soft, comfortable and practical, made in polar fleece fabric. This style is great for everyday winter wear – I like to think of it as a smart alternative to a beanie.

you will need

✱ 18in (46cm) of polar fleece fabric for hat

✱ piece of iron-on fusible web approx. 5in (13cm) x 4in (10cm) for bow centre

cutting out

✱ Cut 2 x piece Ⓐ (front) from main fabric (back to back) or wrong sides together

✱ Cut 2 x piece Ⓑ (back) from main fabric (back to back) or wrong sides together

✱ Cut 1 x piece Ⓒ (band) on fold from main fabric

✱ Cut 2 x piece Ⓓ (bow) on fold from main fabric

✱ Cut 1 x piece Ⓔ (bow) centre from main fabric

✱ Cut 1 x piece Ⓔ (bow) centre from fusible web

102

making up instructions

Step 1

Transfer marker points for tucks on front and back pieces using tailor's tacks, chalk or pins. Also mark the front sections with a pin so that you can easily identify which is the front and which is the back of the hat.

Step 2

Stitch the two backs **B** together at the centre back seam (as marked on pattern template **B** leaving a ½in (13mm) seam allowance (**A**). Press open.

Step 3

Stitch the two fronts **A** together at the centre front seam (as marked on pattern template **A** leaving a ½in (13mm) seam allowance (**B**). Press open.

Step 4

Join front and back sections in a continuous seam from one side to the other. Make tucks in the hat by bringing together the 'x' tuck marks and pinning them. Stitch tucks all around hat top in a continuous seam. The tuck should be approx. ½in (13mm) deep all round (**C**).

Step 5

Stitch the centre back seam in the hatband **C**, leaving a seam allowance of about ¾in (2cm) (**D**). You may wish to try the hatband around your head for size at this stage and make the seam bigger or smaller to fit. Press the seam open. Fold the band in half *wrong* sides together so that raw edges are even. Sew raw edges together all round band approx ½in (13mm) from the raw edge.

Step 6

Turn the hat *inside out*. Pin the band to the hat so that the eventual *outside of the band* is against the *inside of the hat*. Match centre back seam in hat and centre back seam in band. Pin then stitch hat and band together, leaving a ½in (13mm) seam allowance (**E**).

Step 7

Turn the band to the outside of the hat. **NB: The seam allowance will now be sandwiched between the band and the hat on the outside, but will not be seen because it is hidden under the band.**

Step 8

Make the bow. Pin and stitch two bow pieces **D** with right sides together around outside edge, leaving a ½in (13mm) seam allowance. Leave a gap of about 1¼in (3cm) at the lower edge to turn the bow through. Clip into

A

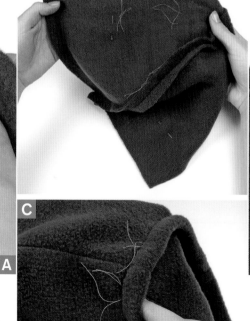

B

C

D

seam allowance and corners. Make bow centre by ironing fusible web to wrong side of centrepiece **E** and folding long edges (marked with a dotted line on pattern piece) to the centre. Fuse in place (**F**).

Step 9

Stitch the two short ends of the bow centre together, right sides together and raw edges even, leaving a ½in (13mm) seam allowance (**G**). Turn right side out. Turn main bow right side out, slip stitch gap in seam and then press lightly. Run a gathering stitch up the centre of the turned bow and pull gathers up, securing the thread at one end.

variations

If the large bow is not to your taste, you could try making a big fleece flower or rosette to trim the side of the hat instead of the front. I have also made this style edged with velvet ribbon at the top of the band and with a cluster of handmade felt leaves in autumnal tones. Although I have used a neutral tone for this hat, it looks stunning made up in a brighter colour such as red. Simply changing the embellishment gives this hat a totally different and more up-to-date feel.

Step 10

Feed gathered bow through centre and arrange so that the centrepiece is in the middle of the bow, covering the gathers.

Step 11

Hand-stitch the bow to the centre front of the hatband. Secure it in place with a few stitches either side of the bow centre and at both bow points (**H**).

1950s

making **vintage** accessories

molly

1950s PURITAN-STYLE FAKE-FUR COLLAR

Detachable collars were a common feature of 1950s fashions. Several sewing patterns from the 1930s to the 1950s featured either a set of different collars or an array of matching belts, collars and dickeys to make.

In the 1950s, many collars were made from lightweight fabrics that allowed home sewers to ring the changes with blouses and dresses. I have designed this one in a familiar 1950s shape but in fake fur to jazz up a winter wardrobe – more practical for today's fashions.

This particular collar has a loop and vintage-button fastening and it is backed with soft wool fabric to prevent it from moving around too much. It could add a touch of glamour to a plain wool jacket or knitted coat and it also offers a stylish, cosy alternative to a winter scarf.

one size

pattern pieces

page 171

suggested fabrics

for collar:
fake fur

for backing and loop:
soft wool flannel

you will need

* 18in (46cm) of fake fur, 25in (64cm) wide for collar

* 18in (46cm) of wool flannel or similar, 25in (64cm) wide for backing and loop

* 1 vintage button, approx 1¼in (3cm) diameter

* blunt needle or bodkin

cutting out

* Cut 1 x piece **A** (collar front/back) on fold from fur fabric

* Cut 1 x piece **A** (collar front/back) on fold from backing fabric

* Cut a strip of wool flannel on the bias (cross-grain), approx 3in (8cm) by 2in (5cm) for the button loop

making up instructions

Step 1
Fold the button loop strip in half lengthways, pin and stitch a seam approx. ¼in (6mm) from the **folded** edge (**A**). Leave two long tails of thread at one end of the seam. Trim the excess fabric away so that the seam allowance is only ¼in (6mm).

Step 2
Thread the two tails of thread through the eye of either a large blunt needle or a bodkin. Next thread the bodkin back through the loop and out through the other end. Use the thread to gently pull on and turn the loop right side out (**B**). (If you have a loop turner you could use this instead.)

Step 3
Fold the loop in half and try it round the button for size. It should fit comfortably around the button when stretched slightly. Also allow

a seam allowance of just over ¼in (6mm) at each end of the loop.

Step 4
Positioned at the right-hand side of the collar, on the right side of the fur fabric, stitch the loop to the collar approx ½in (13mm) from the upper raw edge. The ends of the loop should be lying side by side with the raw ends even with the raw edge of the fur (**C**).

Step 5
With right sides together, pin the fur section of the collar to the collar backing section. The loop will be sandwiched in between the layers. Pin all round with pins at right angles to the raw edge. If you sew carefully, you can leave the pins in while you stitch to help prevent the fur from 'walking' as you sew. Stitch round entire outside edge of collar from lower back, leaving a ½in (4cm) seam

allowance, but remember to leave a gap at the lower centre back of about 1½in (38mm) to turn the collar through (**D**).

Step 6
Clip into the seam allowance round curved edges and clip corners (**E**). Turn the collar right side out through the gap you left at the back. Poke corners using the blunt end of a pencil and smooth curves through the gap before slipstitching the gap closed.

Step 7
Pick the fur out of the seam all round using a blunt needle or bodkin. You can press the collar very lightly from the back, but try to avoid squashing the pile on the fur.

Step 8
Stitch button on left-hand side of collar opposite the loop (**F**).

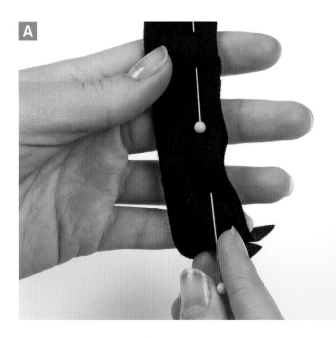

This collar could be made with two velvet ribbon ties instead of the button and loop closure. For added glamour, try making a matching corsage in felt and tweed to pin at one side. Although the collar is an accessory, using the right fur and trims can render it a fashion statement in its own right.

C

E

D

F

stella

1950s SHAPED-BOW LEATHER BELT WITH VINTAGE BUTTON

belt dimensions

The template provided is for a finished belt that measures 31in (79cm) when done up. It should be made to sit slightly below the waist. See tip box for instructions on making a larger version of this belt.

pattern pieces

A B C D

page 172

suggested fabrics

for belt:
suede or leather

for backing:
felt

Belts were an important fashion accessory throughout several decades of the 20th century. Many home sewing patterns offered packages of belts ranging from simple and straight to ornamental and shaped, and some dress or suit patterns included instructions for matching belts.

Many of the waistlines of garments in the 30s, 40s and 50s were defined or accentuated with a sash, buckled or tie-fastening belt, with some even featuring pockets, purses or jewelled trims.

This belt was inspired by a 1950s dressmaking pattern that I found for a collection of 'fascia and contour' belts. I have designed my version to sit nicely just below the waist in keeping with modern fashions.

you will need

* 36in (92cm) by 10in (26cm) of leather or suede for belt and bow trim
* 36in (92cm) by 10in (26cm) of felt for backing
* 36in (92cm) by 10in (26cm) of fusible web
* 2½in (6cm) of Velcro
* 1 vintage button approx 1¼in (3cm) diameter
* hole punch

cutting out

* Cut 1 x piece **A** (belt) on fold from leather or suede
* Cut 1 x piece **A** (belt) on fold from felt
* Cut 1 x piece **A** (belt) on fold from fusible web

* Cut 1 x piece **B** (bow bottom) from leather or suede
* Cut 1 x piece **B** (bow bottom) from felt
* Cut 1 x piece **B** (bow bottom) from fusible web
* Cut 1 x piece **C** (bow middle) from leather or suede
* Cut 1 x piece **C** (bow middle) from felt
* Cut 1 x piece **C** (bow middle) from fusible web
* Cut 1 x piece **D** (bow top) from leather or suede
* Cut 1 x piece **D** (bow top) from leather felt
* Cut 1 x piece **D** (bow top) from fusible web

making up instructions

NB: Before starting this project, refer to Leather, page 15, for tips on how to work with leather.

Step 1

Cut out all pieces **(A)** to **(D)** in leather, felt and fusible web. Iron fusible-web pieces to all felt pieces and peel off paper backing (**A**).

Step 2

Lay the fusible-web-backed felt pieces on top of the leather pieces and fuse together by ironing from the felt side.

Step 3

Machine-stitch around the entire outside edge of each bow section about ¼in (6mm) from the edge. Stitch from the felt side and use a long stitch length.

Step 4

Make two holes in centre of each bow section using a hole punch. They should be about ¼in (6mm) apart, one above each other (**B**).

Step 5

Stack the bow pieces on top of each other: **(B)** on the bottom, **(C)** in the middle and **(D)** on top.) Hand-sew them together through the holes and sew the button in the centre at the same time (**C**).

Step 6

Machine-stitch around the entire outside edge of the main belt piece about ¼in (6mm) from the edge. Stitch from the felt side and use a long stitch length.

Step 7

Pin the Velcro at each end of the belt so that it is level with the raw edges all round (**D**). At one end of the belt, the Velcro should be on the felt side and at the other end on the leather side. Stitch in place all round edge of Velcro about ⅛in (3mm) from the edge of the Velcro. **NB: you should be able to sew this by machine if the leather is not too thick.**

Step 8

Place the bow in the centre of the belt, hold up the two top layers of the bow and machine-stitch the bottom bow to the belt down both sides of the bottom bow piece (**E**). The stitching line should be 1½in (4cm) long and should be hidden from view under the rest of the bow (**F**).

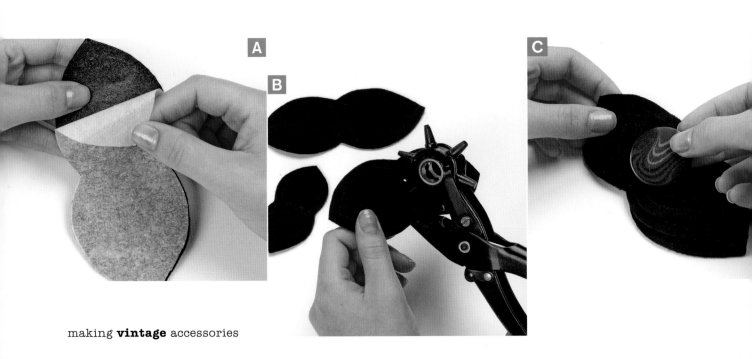

making **vintage** accessories

For a belt up to 6in (15cm) larger, add extra length to
the pattern template at the end marked with a dotted line.
You can make the belt larger either by adding up to 1½in
(4cm) at each end in ½in (13mm) increments. If you want
to add any more than 3in (8cm) overall, then make a break
in the pattern at the line marked with an 'x' at both sides.
Add up to 1in (25mm) either side at that point between
pattern pieces before redrawing. This will help retain the
curved shape of the belt when making the enlargements.

D

F

E

stella.

113

1950s

sylvia

1950s VINTAGE HANDKERCHIEF BOW CORSAGE AND CRAVAT

bow dimensions

Finished bow measures approx 5½in (14cm) by 2in (5cm)

pattern pieces

page 173

suggested fabrics

fine patterned silk fabrics

cravat dimensions

cravat length 32in (81cm)

pattern pieces

page 174

Bows were a popular trim on 1950s fashions and with the current trend for detachable corsages and brooches, a bow corsage makes a pretty vintage-style alternative to the widely available flower versions.

I have a collection of vintage silk handkerchiefs and pieces of scarf fabric that are too small to do anything very elaborate with. Most of them are polka-dot patterned in a variety of colours. Bow corsages fashioned from these hankies lend a delicate vintage touch to a cashmere cardigan. The cravat is a great alternative to a scarf and it stays in place much better. Worn fastened at the front with a neat rose pin it can add a touch of class at the neck of any plain shirt or sweater.

you will need

To make a bow corsage

* 1 large silk handkerchief or a piece of silk measuring 16in (4cm) by 12in (31cm)

* 1 sew-on brooch pin (with holes at the back to stitch through)

* 2 pearl beads (with holes large enough to stitch through)

To make a cravat

* 18in (46cm) of polka-dot patterned silk 36in (92cm) wide.

* fabric rose pin to fasten.

cutting out

* Cut 2 x piece **A** (bow bottom) from silk

* Cut 2 x piece **B** (bow top) from silk

* Cut 1 x piece **C** (bow centre) from silk

cutting out

* Cut 2 x piece **D** (cravat front/back) from silk

making up instructions

to make a bow corsage

Step 1

Pin and stitch together the two bow bottom **A** pieces right sides together round outside edge with a ¼in (6mm) seam allowance and leaving a gap of approx 1½in (4cm) between the 'x' marks at the centre bottom for turning through. Clip into the seam allowance at corners and curved edges (**A**).

Step 2

Turn the bow right side out, then slipstitch the gap closed (**B**). Press the bow bottom well.

Step 3

Pin and stitch the two bow top pieces **B** right sides together round outside edge with ¼in (6mm) seam allowance, leaving a gap of approx 1½in (4cm) between the 'x' marks for turning through. Clip into the seam allowance at corners and curved edges, then turn the bow right side out. Slipstitch opening closed and press.

Step 4

Centre the bow top over the bow bottom and pin. Thread a needle with a double length of thread and run a gathering stitch down the centre of the stacked bow, through both top and bottom layers. Pull up the gathering stitches tightly (**C**) and secure thread at the bottom of the bow.

Step 5

Fold the bow centre piece **C** in half lengthways with right sides together. Stitch along side and both ends, leaving a gap in the centre of the side seam between 'x' marks on pattern template for turning through. Turn right side out, press and stitch gap closed – you can machine-stitch this as it will be on the back of the bow out of sight (**D**).

Step 6

Tie the bow centre around the middle of the gathered bow, covering the gathers (**E**). The end of the tie should be facing opposite ends of the bow. Stitch a pearl bead either side of the bow centre, diagonally opposite each other (**F**).

Step 7

Stitch a brooch pin to the back of the bow through the holes in the pin (**G**).

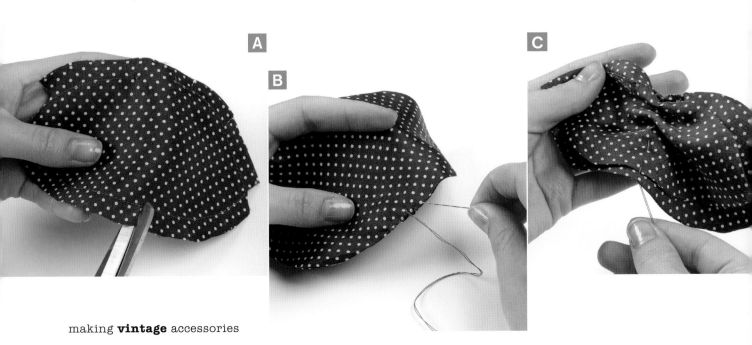

to make a cravat

NB: These instructions are not accompanied by step-by-step photographs, as they follow the same method as most of the book's other scarves and collars, for example, **Celia**, pages 88–91, or **Jean**, pages 132–5.

Step 1

Pin the two cravat pieces right sides together. Stitch around entire outside edge with a ½in (13mm) seam allowance, but leaving a gap of about 2in (5cm) at the centre back between 'x' marks to turn the cravat through.

Step 2

Clip into the seam allowance at corners and curved edges and then turn the cravat right side out through the gap. Push out cravat corners using the blunt end of a pencil, then slipstitch gap closed and press cravat thoroughly.

sewing tip

The polka dot handkerchiefs I used were 18in (46cm) square and I cut the bow centre **C** from the plain strip around the edge of the hanky. Small vintage headscarves would also be good for this purpose, as they usually have a plain border around the outside.

Step 3

Stitch a small brooch pin to the back of a handmade or purchased ribbon rose. Wear the cravat tied at the front so that the ends sit on top of each other and pin in place with the rose.

sylvia.

117

1950s

making **vintage** accessories

1960s

cynthia

1960s LARGE COLOUR-BLOCKED OVAL-BASED BAG

bag dimensions

Approximately 13in (33cm)
wide by 11½in (29cm) tall
(excluding handle); gusset
depth 3in (8cm); handle 24in
(61cm) long

pattern pieces

A B C D

E F G

pages 175–8

suggested fabrics

for main bag:
wool flannel/tweed or cotton
prints in three toning colours

for lining:
fancy patterned silk or cotton

This pattern offers a large functional bag in a striking colour-blocked design reminiscent of 1960s fabrics. It resembles the popular 'bucket' bags of the era and, although I have used neutral colours, you could try bolder and brighter combinations and prints for a more psychedelic 1960s look.

The bag is deep with a set-in base to give it a roomy three-dimensional shape and the shoulder strap makes it a versatile all-rounder. A row of three big buttons sewn on the long flap finishes off the simple statement.

you will need

* 18in (46cm) of wool fabric, 36in (92cm) wide for base, lower front/back and handle

* 8in (20cm) of wool fabric, 36in (92cm) wide for middle front/back

* 13in (33cm) of wool fabric, 36in (92cm) wide for top front/back and flap

* 18in (46cm) of quilted calico, 45in (114cm) wide for interfacing

* 18in (46cm) of patterned silk or cotton, 45in (114cm) wide for lining

* piece of iron-on interfacing, approx 10in (26cm) by 12in (31cm) for flap

* 3 buttons, approx 1¼in (3cm) diameter for flap trim

* 1 piece 1½in (4cm) square of craft interfacing (for snap stabilizer on bag front)

* magnetic snap set

cutting out

* Cut 2 x piece **A** (top front/back) on fold from main fabric 1

* Cut 2 x piece **B** (middle front/back) on fold from main fabric 2

* Cut 2 x piece **C** (lower front/back) on fold from main fabric 3

* Cut 2 x piece **D** (front/back lining) on fold from lining fabric

* Cut 2 x piece **D** (front/back lining) on fold from interfacing

* Cut 1 x piece **E** (base) on fold from main fabric 3

* Cut 1 x piece **E** (base) on fold from interfacing

* Cut 1 x piece **E** (base) on fold from lining fabric

* Cut 2 x piece **F** (flap) on fold from main fabric 1

* Cut 2 x piece **F** (flap) on fold from iron-on interfacing

* Cut 1 x piece **G** (handle) on fold from main fabric 3

* Cut 1 x piece **G** (handle) on fold from iron-on interfacing

making up instructions

Step 1

Stitch top front/back pieces **A** to pieces from the middle front/back **B** along edges marked with a slashed line on pattern templates. Leave ½in (13mm) seam allowance (**A**). Stitch lower front/back sections **C** to middle sections **B** along edges with dotted line on pattern templates. Leave ½in (13mm) seam allowance. Press all seams open flat (**B**).

Step 2

Pin assembled bag front/back to corresponding front/back interfacing pieces and baste together (**C**). Refer to **Sew-in Interfacing**, page 17. Transfer snap marker onto middle front and attach magnetic half of snap, referring to **How to Apply a Magnetic Snap**, page 18.

Step 3

With right sides together, stitch front and back sections together down side seams, leaving a ½in (13mm) seam allowance. Clip into seam allowance at curves.

Step 4

Pin bag base **E** to corresponding base interfacing piece **E** and baste together, referring to **Sew-in Interfacing**, page 17. Pin bag base to bag front/back at lower edge. Match 'x' marks with side seams (**D**). Stitch with a ½in (13mm) seam allowance. Clip into the seam allowance around curved edges. Turn bag right side out.

Step 5

Make flap. Iron interfacing to wrong side of flap pieces **F** . Transfer the magnetic snap position marker onto one of the flap pieces and fix non-magnetic half of snap. Refer to **How to Apply a Magnetic Snap**, page 18.

Step 6

Pin flap pieces right sides together. Stitch together round sides/lower edges, leaving ½in (13mm) seam allowance. Trim away excess bulk, clip into seam allowance at lower curved edge and turn right sides out. Press flat, topstitch all round using a longer stitch length (**E**).

Step 7

Pin the finished flap to the back of the bag centrally, right outside of flap against right outside of bag back, with raw edges even. Baste, using a long stitch length, approx. ½in (13mm) from the edge.

Step 8

Make handle by ironing interfacing onto reverse side of handle piece **G** , folding in long edges to centre, then folding in half lengthways again and topstitching together down open side and again along closed side. Refer to section on **Self-fabric Handles**, page 20.

Step 9

On outside of bag, positioned centred over side seams with raw edges even, pin handle to bag and baste in place. Refer to **Attaching Long Handles to Bags**, page 20.

Step 10

Stitch front and back lining sections **D** right sides together down side seams, using a ½in (13mm) seam allowance. Pin base

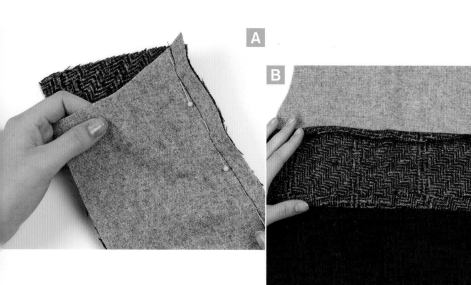

lining  to bag front/back lining at lower edge, matching 'x' marks with side seams. Stitch with a ½in (13mm) seam allowance. Leave a gap of about 4in (10cm) in the seam at one side of base to turn bag through.

Step 11

Insert bag into lining with right sides together. Pin bag and lining together through all thicknesses round upper edges, having raw edges even. Stitch through all thicknesses, using a normal stitch length and leaving a seam allowance of just over ½in (13mm). Trim seam back to ⅜in (1cm) and clip into seam allowance at sides.

Step 12

Turn the bag through the opening in the bottom of the lining and push the lining to the inside of the bag. Refer to **To Line the Bags in this Book**, page 22. Roll the lining with your fingers so that it is not visible from the outside and pin it in place all round top, ensuring that the flap will sit correctly. Topstitch through all layers, about ½in

variations

This bag is one of the largest in the book and it lends itself well to piecing with contrasting or patterned fabrics of all kinds. Try using different decorator fabrics in retro prints for each section, resulting in a more marked contrast between blocks – and still a durable bag.

You may wish to include a simple pocket on the inside of this bag. I used a piece of beautiful woven silk fabric to line my example and added an internal pocket made from a double rectangle of silk (**G**). Remember to stitch the pocket to the back lining piece before you assemble the bag lining.

(13mm) from the top of the bag, using a long stitch length.

Step 13

Slipstitch the opening in the lining closed, tuck lining back into bag and give the bag a final press with a cloth. Press first with flap open and then again with flap closed.

If necessary, to secure the lining into the bag further, you can hand-stitch a few stitches at the side seams, through bag and lining.

Step 14

Stitch three buttons down the flap as decoration (**F**).

cynthia

1960s

making **vintage** accessories

bag dimensions

Approximately 10in (26cm)
wide by 9½in (24cm) tall
(excluding handle); handle
17½in (44cm) long

pattern pieces

pages 179–81

suggested fabrics

for main bag fabric:
wool flannel/tweed

for bag flap:
fancy patterned cotton

124

sophia

1960s VASE-SHAPED HANDBAG WITH POCKET

The modern 'vase' shape of this bag has simple yet elegant curves. The pocket adds texture and interest to the front, while the asymmetric handle with a metal ring adds a modern feel with retro 1960s appeal. The bright colour is also very eye-catching.

This bag is a reasonable size to use for almost any occasion and can be made up in everything from plain or fancy wools to brocade, velvet and silk for a funky look. A cotton lining in a vintage-style print finishes it off perfectly.

you will need

* 18in (46cm) of wool fabric, 36in (92cm) wide for bag
* 14in (36cm) of lining fabric, 36in (92cm) for lining
* 14in (36cm) of quilted calico, 36in (92cm) for interfacing
* iron-on interfacing 36in (92cm) by 5in (13cm) for handle and pocket top
* 1 metal ring approx 1½in (4cm) diameter for handle
* piece of plastic canvas or stiff card 6in (15cm) by 2in (5cm) for base
* 2 pieces x 1½in (4cm) square of craft interfacing (for snap stabilizers)
* 1 magnetic snap set
* optional cover button badge trim from **Marianne**, pages 136–9.

cutting out

* Cut 2 x piece **A** (front/back) from main fabric (cut right wrong sides together)
* Cut 2 x piece **A** (front/back) from interfacing (cut right wrong sides together)
* Cut 2 x piece **A** (front/back) from lining fabric (cut right wrong sides together)
* Cut 1 x piece **B** (pocket) on fold from main fabric
* Cut 1 x piece **C** (pocket band) from main fabric
* Cut 1 x piece **C** (pocket band) from iron-on interfacing
* Cut 1 x piece **D** (pocket lining) on fold from lining fabric
* Cut 1 x piece **E** (handle) on fold from main fabric
* Cut 1 x piece **E** (handle) on fold from iron-on interfacing
* Cut 1 x piece **F** (handle tab) from main fabric
* Cut 1 x piece **F** (handle tab) from iron-on interfacing

making up instructions

Step 1

Pin the bag front/back **A** to the corresponding front/back interfacing pieces **A**, and baste together round the entire outside edge. Refer to **Sew-in Interfacing**, page 17.

Step 2

Form pleats in pocket piece **B** by bringing lines together and pinning in place (**A**). Stitch pleats in place along upper edge and press pleats towards the centre of the pocket on the right side.

Step 3

Iron interfacing to the wrong side of the pocket band **C**. Fold band in half lengthways and press (**B**). Stitch pleated edge of pocket to one side of the band. Stitch pocket lining **D** to the other side of the band but leave a gap of approx. 1½in (4cm) for turning the pocket through (**C**).

Step 4

Fold the assembled pocket in half with right sides together. Stitch in a continuous line from top of band to top of band on other side, leaving a ½in (13mm) seam allowance (**D**). Turn pocket right side out through the gap you left, then slipstitch gap closed (**E**). Press pocket.

Step 5

Lay the pocket on the front piece at position shown on bag front pattern piece (**F**). Topstitch in place approx. ¼in (6mm) from the edge (**G**) and press pocket lightly.

Step 6

Pin the front/back pieces right sides together. Stitch together at side and lower edges, leaving the corners free. Fold the lower corners of the bag matching seams, and stitch straight across to form gusset. For help with this step refer to **Assembling the Bag**, page 19. Clip seam allowance along curved edges, turn bag right side out and press lightly.

Step 7

Iron interfacing onto reverse side of handle piece **E** and fold in long raw edges to centre. Fold handle in half lengthways and topstitch together down open side and again along closed side, approx. ¼in (6mm) from edges. Refer to section on **Self-fabric Handles**, page 20. Iron interfacing to reverse side of handle tab **F** and fold edges marked with a dotted line to centre. Fold tab in half lengthways and topstitch together down open side and again along closed side, approx. ¼in (6mm) from edges.

Step 8

Wrap handle tab around metal ring and stitch ends together, keeping raw edges of tab even. Wrap the

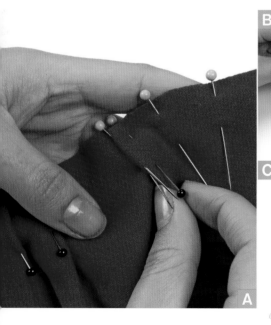

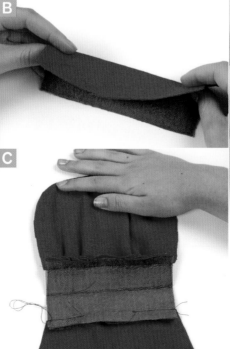

long handle around the other side of the metal ring, tuck raw edge under and hand-sew in place at both sides and along the top. On outside of the bag, positioned centred over side seams with raw edges even, pin completed handle to bag and baste in place. Refer to **Attaching Long Handles to Bags**, page 20. Attach with the ring side of handle at the right of the bag (**H**).

Step 9

Transfer the magnetic snap position markers onto the bag lining front/ back and fix magnetic snap so that both pieces are opposite each other. Refer to **How to Apply a Magnetic Snap**, page 18.

Step 10

Stitch front and back lining pieces **A** together, with right sides together. Stitch together at side and lower edges, leaving corners

free. Leave a gap in the seam at the bottom of about 4in (10cm) for turning the bag through. Fold the lower corners of the bag matching seams and stitch straight across to form gusset.

Step 11

Insert bag into lining with right sides together. Pin bag and lining together through all thicknesses round upper edges, keeping raw edges even. Stitch through all thicknesses using a normal stitch length and leaving a seam allowance of just over ½in (13mm). Trim seam back to ⅜in (1cm) and clip into the seam allowance at sides. Clip seam at top of bag *all round* as this is a curved edge.

Step 12

Turn the bag right side out through the opening in the bottom of lining and push the lining to the inside of the bag. Refer to **To Line the Bags**

in this Book, page 22. Roll the lining with your fingers so that it is not visible from the outside and pin it in place all round top. Topstitch through all layers, about ½in (13mm) from the top of the bag, using a long stitch length.

Step 13

Insert a piece of plastic canvas or some thick card into the bottom of the bag through the opening in the lining to give shape to the base of the bag. Slipstitch the opening in the lining closed, tuck lining back into bag and give the bag a final press under a cloth.

Step 14

If you want, you can make a cover button badge to pin on the bag, following instructions in **Marianne**, pages 136–9.

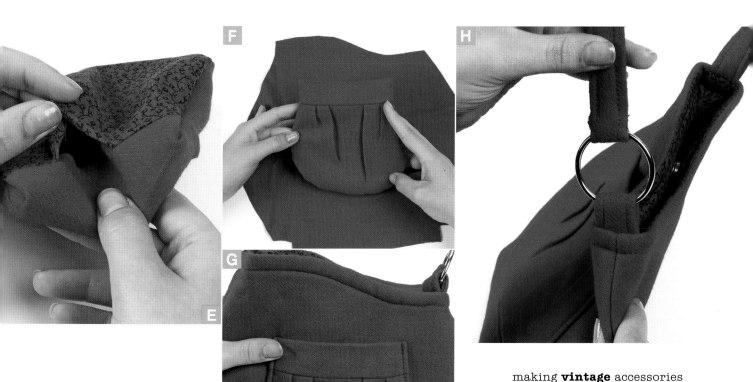

making **vintage** accessories

daphne

1960s FLEECE CAP WITH BOW TAB TRIM

People tend to think of caps as quite a modern fashion, but hats with peaks were popular with women as far back as the 1940s. I have designed this jaunty cap in keeping with the 1960s theme but with an earlier construction method.

Made from just three main pattern pieces, the cap works well in soft stretchy fleece, giving the smart appearance of wool, but it is much easier to work with.

The tab I have used at the front, which would also work well on the flap of a clutch bag, gives a vaguely military feel to the cap, which is again in keeping with 1960s–era fashions.

hat dimensions

To fit a medium-size head measurement of approx 22in (56cm)

pattern pieces

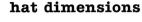

pages 181–3

suggested fabrics

for cap:
polar fleece

for lining:
patterned cotton

you will need

* 18in (46cm) of polar fleece, 45in (114cm) wide

* 14in (36cm) of lining fabric 36in (92cm) wide

* piece of iron-on interfacing, 20in (51cm) by 12in (31cm) for peak and tab

* piece of stiffener for peak, 10in (26cm) by 10in (26cm) (craft weight interfacing would do)

* approx 24in (61cm) of grosgrain ribbon, 1in (25mm) width for band

* piece of fusible web, approx. 6in (15cm) by 3in (8cm) for bow centre

* 2 x cover buttons, approx 1in (25mm) diameter for tab trim

cutting out

* Cut 1 x piece **A** (side/back) on fold from main fabric

* Cut 1 x piece **A** (side/back) on fold from lining fabric

* Cut 1 x piece **B** (top/front) on fold from main fabric

* Cut 1 x piece **B** (top/front) on fold from lining fabric

* Cut 2 x piece **C** (peak) on fold from main fabric

* Cut 2 x piece **C** (peak) on fold from iron-on interfacing

* Cut 1 x piece **C** (peak) on fold from stiff interfacing

* Cut 1 x piece **D** (tab front) on fold from main fabric

* Cut 1 x piece **E** (tab back) on fold from main fabric

* Cut 1 x piece **E** (tab back) on fold from iron-on interfacing

* Cut 1 x piece **F** (tab centre) from main fabric

* Cut 1 x piece **F** (tab centre) from fusible web

making up instructions

Step 1

Stitch cap top/front section **B** to side/back section **A** along edges marked with a dashed line on pattern templates, matching the large dot and 'x' markers. Using fleece fabric will make it easier to stitch around the curved sections (**A**). Leave a ½in (13mm) seam allowance. Push the seam allowance toward the centre of the cap and topstitch in place, about ¼in (6mm) from the seam all round. Turn cap right side out.

Step 2

Stitch cap top/front lining **B** to side/back lining **A** along edges marked with a dashed line on pattern templates, matching the large dot and 'x' markers. Leave a ½in (13mm) seam allowance as for main cap.

Step 3

Insert lining into cap with wrong sides together and pin, matching

all seams and with raw edges even (**B**). Stitch together about ½in (13mm) from the raw edge. Neaten the seam allowance with a zigzag machine stitch or overlocker.

Step 4

Iron interfacing on to wrong sides of both peak **C** sections. Then with right sides together, stitch peaks together around edge marked with a dashed line on pattern template, leaving a ½in (13mm) seam allowance. Trim seam allowance back to cut down on bulk and clip curves (**C**). Turn peak right side out and press.

Step 5

Take the peak cut from stiffener and trim about ½in (13mm) from all round curved edge so that it will fit inside the peak. Insert cut stiffener piece into peak so it sits underneath seam allowance on under side of peak (**D**). Pin stiffener in place and stitch raw

edges of peak together, catching in the stiffener. Topstitch peak, first ½in (13mm) from outside edge, then twice more spaced ½in (13mm) apart.

Step 6

Pin peak to the cap right sides together with peak facing upwards so that the centre of the peak is matched with the cap centre front. Stitch peak to cap, leaving a ½in (13mm) seam allowance. Clip into the seam allowance to free up the curved edge.

Step 7

Try cap on to ascertain sizing. Pin grosgrain to the cap, covering the seam and zigzagging (refer to **Hats**, page 24, for help with this step). **NB: You will be pinning it over the peak at the front, too**. If the cap is a bit large, take in a little of the fullness when pinning in the grosgrain, so that the hat will be tighter (or see **Sewing Tip**).

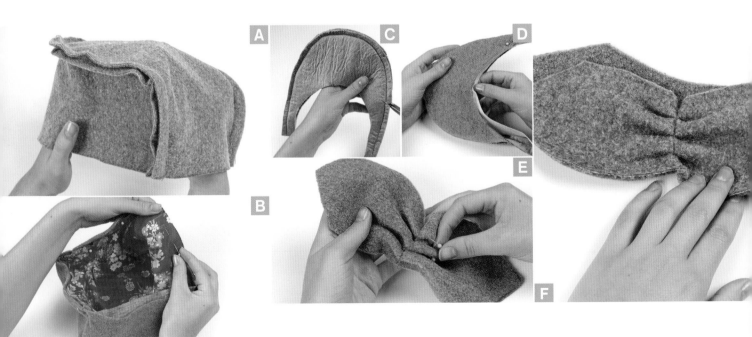

Step 8

Fold one end of the ribbon over, and overlap the two ends of the ribbon with the folded edge on top. Stitch the ribbon in place about ¼in (6mm) from upper edge of grosgrain. Stitch folded end of grosgrain ribbon to itself. Turn the ribbon upwards and stitch with a few hand-stitches to the cap lining.

Step 9

Make the tab. Make three pleats in the centre of the tab front **D** by bringing together pleat lines on the wrong side of the tab front and pinning in place. Stitch pleats in place down centre of tab (**E**).

Step 10

Iron interfacing to wrong side of tab back piece **E**. With right sides together pin tab front to tab back. You must push the fullness of top section toward the tab's middle so raw edges of top and bottom sections are even (**F**).

As with all hats, sizing can be a problem. This can be alleviated by making the seams slightly bigger or smaller or adjusting the grosgrain fractionally in most cases. However, with this cap, because the back is quite soft and there are no brims/peaks there, after you have completed most of Step 8 but **before** you turn the grosgrain up, you could add a short piece of elastic (about 2in/5cm long).

Stitch together ¼in (6mm) from raw edge, leaving gap of about 1in (25mm) at lower edge to turn tab through. Clip into seam allowance and at corners, then turn right side out through gap (**G**). Slipstitch gap closed then press lightly.

Step 11

Make the tab centre by ironing fusible web to the reverse of the tab centre piece **F** and folding in the long edges marked with a dashed line on the pattern template to the centre. Fuse in place. Stitch the two short ends of the tab centre together, right sides together and raw edges

even, leaving a ½in (13mm) seam allowance. Turn the right side out (**H**).

Step 12

Feed tab through tab centre and arrange so that the tab centre is in the middle of the tab (**I**).

Step 13

Hand-stitch the tab to the centre front of the cap so that it sits just above the peak. Secure tab to the cap with a few stitches at the top and bottom of the tab centre and at both points. Cover two buttons with fleece scraps and stitch one at each end of the tab (**J**).

daphne

131

1960s

making **vintage** accessories

jean

1960s VINTAGE SCARF BELT WITH RING ENDS

Belts were particularly popular in the 1960s in a variety of materials from patent leather to plastic, often with ornamental buckles or unusual methods of closure.

Belts are a very useful fashion addition to any wardrobe. Adding a bold, wide belt to a simple dress, or a skinny belt with diamante trim to a favourite pair of jeans can transform an outfit from ordinary to chic. Yet, people are often deterred from making belts because of the sizing issue, but creating a belt with tie fastening overcomes this problem. This project offers a simple belt and scarf in one design, which, when combined, make an effective statement. The great thing is that you can ring the changes by wearing different scarves tied through the loops.

you will need

* 18in (46cm) of satin fabric, minimum of 48in (122cm) wide for scarf

* 12in (31cm) of wool fabric, minimum of 36in (92cm) wide for belt

* 12in (31cm) of iron-on interfacing, with minimum of 36in (92cm) wide for belt

* 2 metal rings 1¾in (45mm) diameter for belt ends

* 4 vintage metal buttons for belt trim

scarf cutting out

* To make your complete scarf pattern, enlarge, copy and join pieces **A** (scarf end) and **B** (scarf middle) as directed on pattern pieces, matching 'o' and 'x' marks. Then redraw the pattern on a large piece of paper along either of the edges marked 'fold'. When you cut the scarf out of fabric, place the completed pattern on the fold of the fabric along the other edge marked 'fold'. Cut the scarf out in one piece.

belt cutting out

* Cut 2 x piece **C** (belt front/back) on fold from main fabric

* Cut 2 x piece **C** (belt front/back) on fold from iron-on interfacing

scarf dimensions

The scarf measures 44in (112cm) long (point to point) and is 6½in (16cm) wide.

belt dimensions

The standard template in this project will make a belt that is approx. 34in (86cm) long when done up with the scarf.

A B C

pages 184–5

suggested fabrics

for scarf:
soft silk or satin print

for belt:
wool tweed or flannel, firm cotton (prints or plain)

jean

133

1960s

making up instructions

Step 1
Fold scarf in half lengthways with right sides together. Pin and stitch, leaving ½in (13mm) seam allowance, from point at one end along open edge and to other pointed end, leaving a gap of about 2in (5cm) to turn the scarf through (**A**) at the centre back.

Step 2
Clip the corners of scarf seam allowance (**B**). Turn scarf right side out through gap (**C**). Push out scarf corners using blunt end of a pencil, then slipstitch gap closed and press scarf seam thoroughly.

Step 3
Iron interfacing to wrong side of both belt pieces **C** . Place belt pieces right sides together, raw edges even. Stitch together round outside edges with ½in (13mm) seam allowance. Leave gap of 2in (5cm) at centre back lower edge of belt through which to turn it (**D**).

Step 4
Trim the seam allowance back to about ¼in (6mm) to cut down on bulk (**E**) and clip into seam allowance at curved edges and corners. Turn belt right side out through the gap (**F**). Do not worry if the belt is slightly twisted – it will flatten out when you press it. Push out corners, shape curved edges and press the belt flat, then slipstitch gap closed. Topstitch around the entire outside edge of the belt about ¼in (6mm) from the edge and again ¼in (6mm) from the first line of topstitching.

Step 5
At each end, fold the end of the belt around a metal ring. You should fold over ¾in (2cm) to the wrong side of the belt and then machine-stitch it in place in one continuous line from the top to lower edge of belt. Stitch one or two decorative buttons at each end of the belt (**G**).

Step 6
To do the belt up, loop the scarf through the metal rings at each end and tie in a loose knot (**H**).

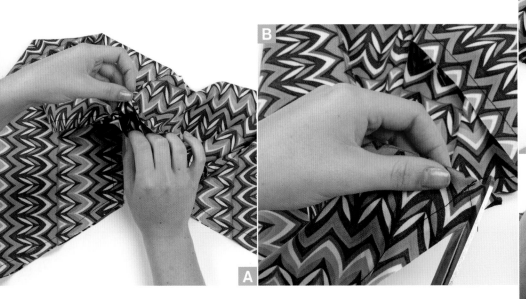

Try making the belt from jazzy tartan, country tweed, tapestry, brocade or even floral and retro prints for summer wear. You could then make or purchase a plain scarf to fasten it with.

Another option would be to make both the scarf and belt from plain fabrics, and instead of trimming with vintage buttons, you could make a rose corsage to trim one side of the belt. You could also use one large vintage button at each end, or substitute the metal rings for colourful vintage Lucite hoops. Small plastic bangles (children's size) are also an option for the ring ends.

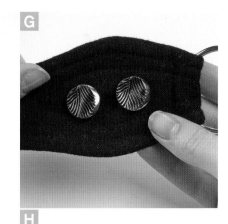

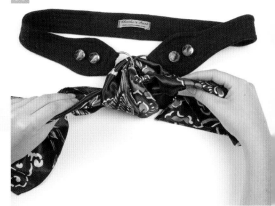

marianne

1960s COVERED BUTTON BADGES

I started making button 'collage' badges because I had so many beautiful scraps of tweed, silk, leather and lace left over from other accessory projects, which seemed far too good to simply throw away.

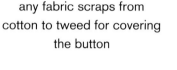

suggested fabrics

any fabric scraps from cotton to tweed for covering the button

While using these small scraps to plan colour schemes for handbags, I discovered that they made rather delightful statements in their own right when made up as badges. Showing them at craft fairs alongside my other wares, people often commented on how nice it was to be able to 'wear' little pieces of fabric art.

Button badges were invented towards the end of the 19th century for use as cost-effective souvenirs, but in their current form they date back to the 1960s, when they were used to convey political opinions and musical preferences. Badges have enjoyed a comeback in recent years, particularly made from vintage fabrics, papers or images.

you will need

* metal cover buttons with removable shanks in a variety of sizes

* fabric to cover the buttons

* brooch bar pins to fit on button backs

* strong glue suitable for metal (such as a two-part epoxy resin)

* selection of ribbon, lace, buttons, feathers etc for trimming

* pliers to remove button shanks

For the red collection shown here, I used a set of vintage Viyella fabric swatches. The badges with words on them can be achieved in several ways. You can transfer words to fabric using T-shirt transfer paper, or you can use a paper-backed fabric that can be fed directly through the computer printer, as I did. I have then cut out the words and stitched them to the centre of the fabric circle using a decorative zigzag stitch.

making up instructions

Step 1
Remove the shank of the button using small pliers (**A**) – squeeze on the loop of the shank and it should come out quite easily.

Step 2
Cut out a circle of your chosen fabric to cover the button. If you buy the buttons in a packet, there is usually a template on the back of the pack that you can use to cut out your fabric so that it fits round the button. You will need the circle to be big enough to fit right round the button, overlap the edges and tuck underneath. Most of the templates are semi-circular. I find it useful to redraw the template on a piece of paper, full circle, and mark the size on it for future reference (**B**).

Step 3
As only the centre of the circle of fabric will be seen on top of the button, it is useful to draw around the outside edge of the actual

button and cut a circle of see-through plastic the same size, to help you plan your design (I cut mine from the plastic top of the button packet). This way, you can be sure how much of your design will show on the finished item (**C**).

Step 4
Stitch any elements that can be machine-sewn to the circle of fabric first, such as ribbons across the centre, joins in the fabric, or braids.

Step 5
Lay out any buttons, lace or three-dimensional elements using your plastic disc to help you plan the design. Once you are happy with the design, hand-stitch these elements in place.

Step 6
Thread a needle with a double thickness of thread and run a gathering stitch around the outside

edge of the now trimmed circle of fabric, about ¼in (6mm) from the raw edge (**D**).

Step 7
Place the button (now minus the shank) in the centre of the circle and pull up the gathering thread tight so that the fabric sits snugly around the button (**E**). Finish off the gathering thread ensuring it is secure, and then cut thread.

Step 8
Snap the back of the button on – you may need to use pliers to help do this, particularly if the fabric is thick (**F**).

Step 9
Finish by gluing a brooch pin to the back of the button. Glue it slightly nearer the top of the button to prevent the badge from hanging down when worn. You may like to glue a small piece of leather or felt over the back of the pin for extra security.

A

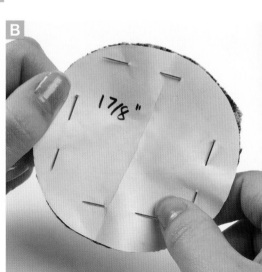

B

17/8 "

C

Collect and co-ordinate small pieces of fabric, buttons and ribbons for badge projects when you have scraps left over from bigger sewing projects. I have even made badges using manufacturers' fabric swatches, including some beautiful tweeds and prints from when I was running my own clothing design business.

variations

These badges offer a great way to use up odd vintage buttons, creating keepsakes as well as fashion accessories. Try making a colour-themed cluster of badges. They can be worn individually, in pairs or as full sets for maximum impact.

In the **pink and brown collection** (left), the large 2in (5cm) badge with the hand-painted lace butterflies is undoubtedly the centre piece. However, I have also made a rickrack flower badge, as in **Clementine**, pages 48–51, in toning colours with a beautiful cut-glass vintage button centre to match.

With the **green collection** (right), I have used more of my wonderful hand-painted lace, scraps of rickrack and a pretty hand-painted rose.

marianne

139

1960s

E

F

enlarge all pattern pieces by 200%

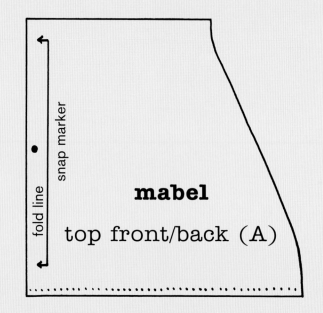

fold line

snap marker

mabel

top front/back (A)

when photocopying, align dotted rule with top edge of glass

mabel **B** **C**

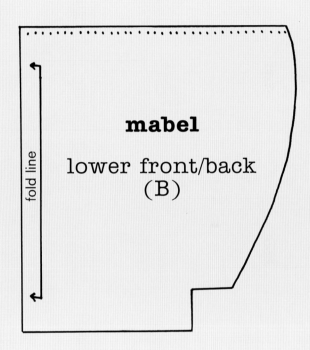

mabel

lower front/back
(B)

fold line

enlarge all pattern
pieces by 200%

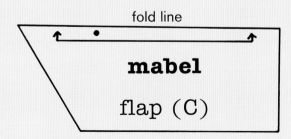

fold line

mabel

flap (C)

mabel

enlarge all pattern pieces by 200%

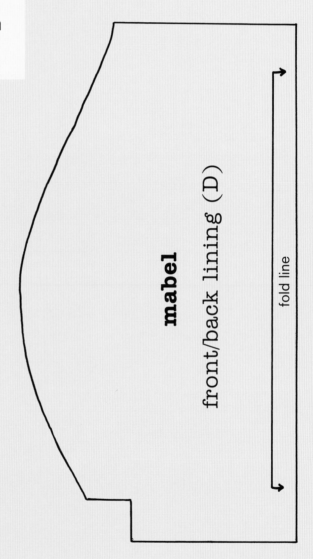

mabel
front/back lining (D)

fold line

pattern templates

when photocopying, align dotted rule with top edge of glass

mabel

enlarge all pattern
pieces by 200%

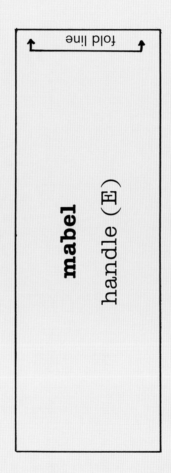

fold line

mabel
handle (E)

making **vintage** *accessories*

ⓐ vita

enlarge all pattern
pieces by 200%

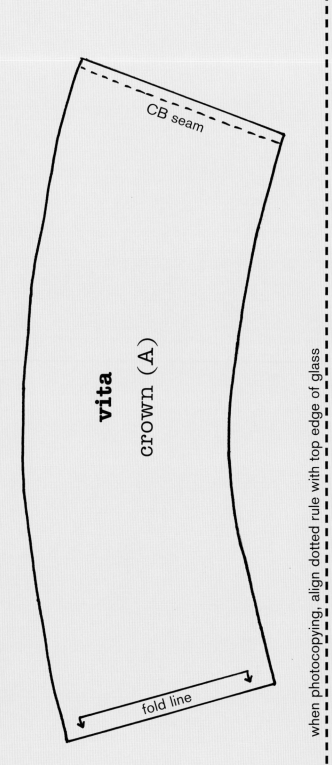

CB seam

vita
crown (A)

fold line

when photocopying, align dotted rule with top edge of glass

vita B C

enlarge all pattern
pieces by 200%

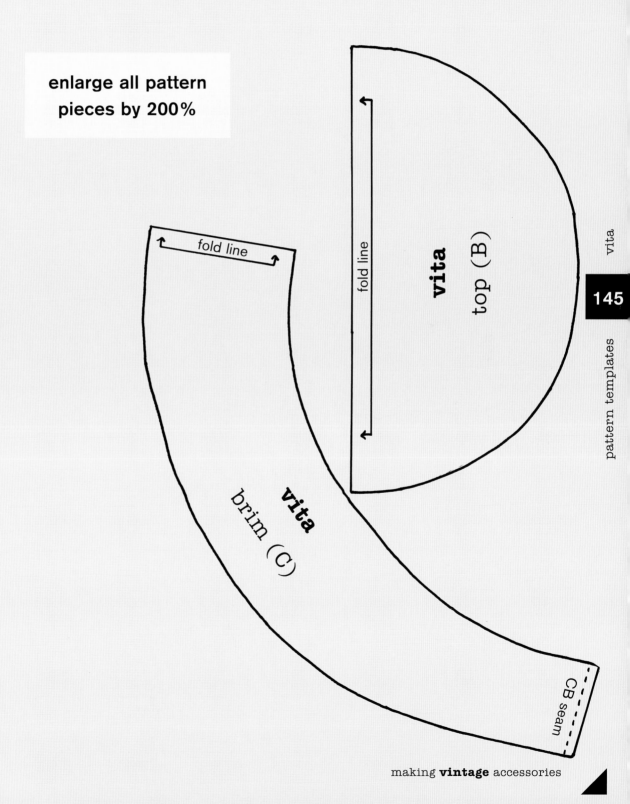

fold line

vita
top (B)

fold line

fold line

vita
brim (C)

CB seam

enlarge all pattern
pieces by 200%

146

pattern templates

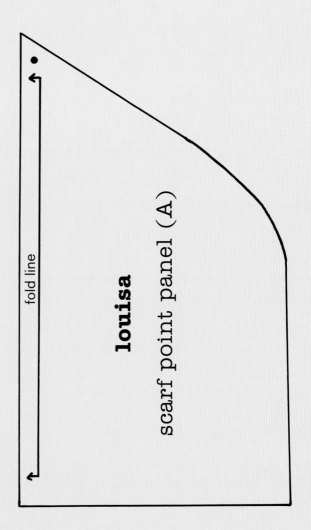

fold line

louisa
scarf point panel (A)

when photocopying, align dotted rule with top edge of glass

enlarge all pattern
pieces by 200%

fold line

louisa
tuck-through panel (B)

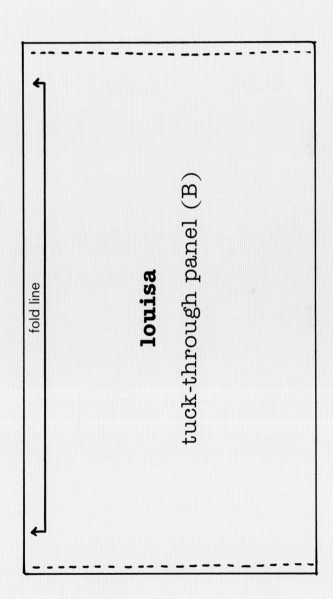

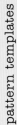

enlarge all pattern pieces by 200%

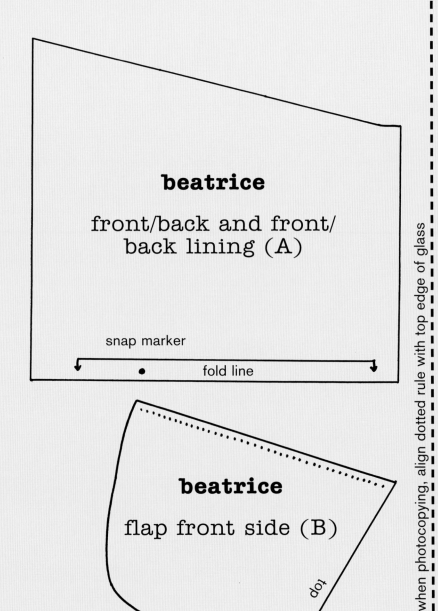

beatrice

front/back and front/ back lining (A)

snap marker

● fold line

beatrice

flap front side (B)

top

when photocopying, align dotted rule with top edge of glass

beatrice C D

enlarge all pattern
pieces by 200%

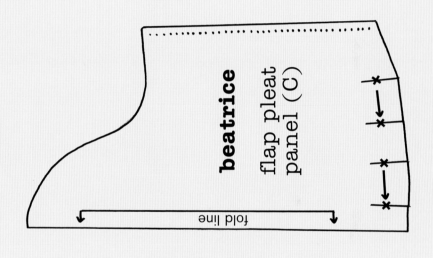

beatrice
flap pleat
panel (C)

fold line

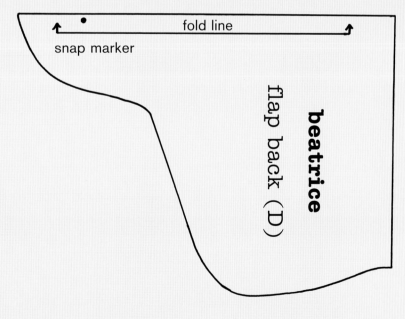

fold line

snap marker

beatrice
flap back (D)

enlarge all pattern
pieces by 200%

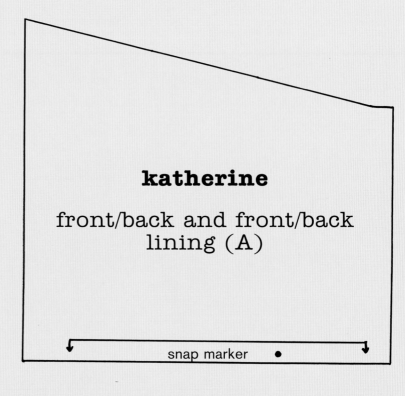

katherine

front/back and front/back
lining (A)

snap marker ●

when photocopying, align dotted rule with top edge of glass

katherine (B)

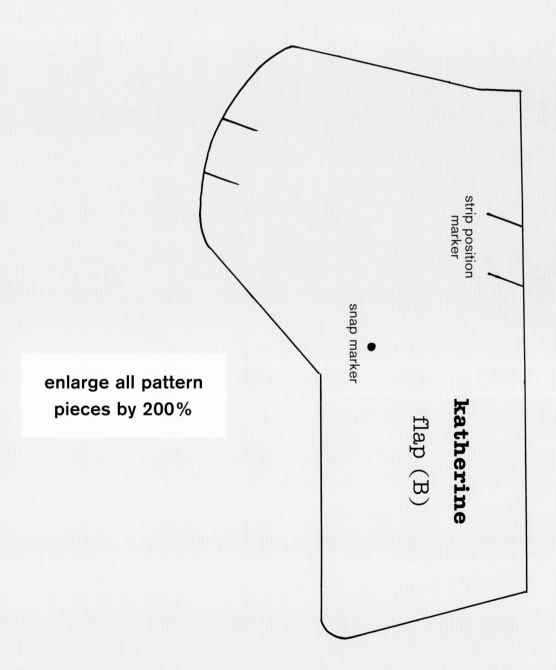

enlarge all pattern
pieces by 200%

strip position
marker

snap marker

•

katherine
flap (B)

enlarge all pattern
pieces by 200%

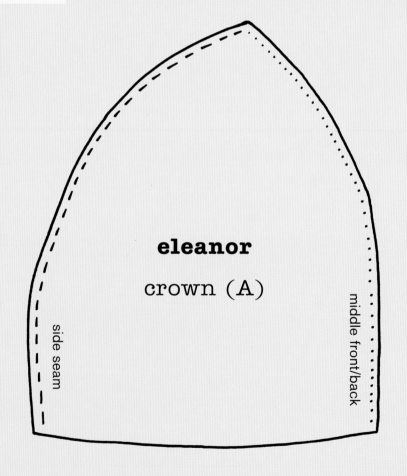

eleanor

crown (A)

side seam

middle front/back

when photocopying, align dotted rule with top edge of glass

eleanor B C

enlarge all pattern
pieces by 200%

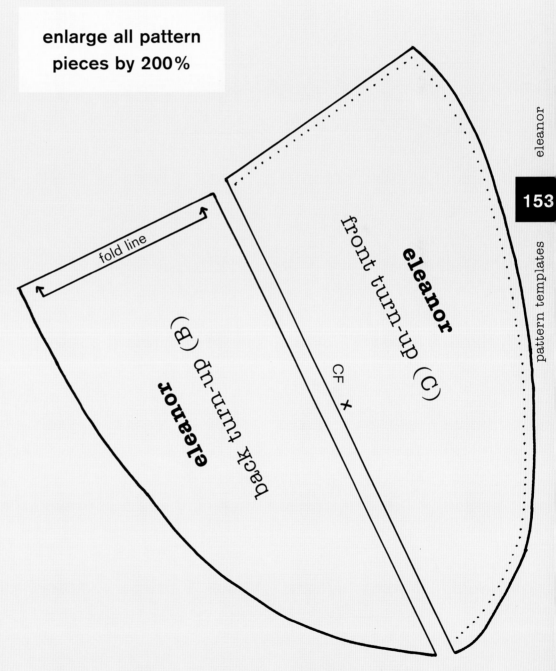

fold line

eleanor
back turn-up (B)

eleanor
front turn-up (C)

CF
×

Ⓐ jessica

Ⓐ Ⓑ Ⓒ deborah

enlarge all pattern
pieces by 200%

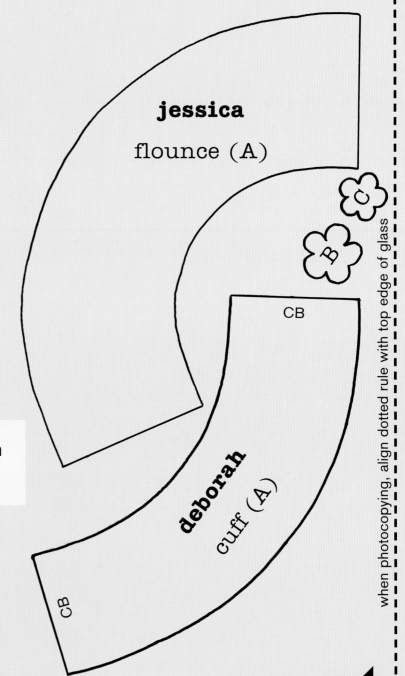

jessica

flounce (A)

Ⓒ

Ⓑ

CB

deborah

cuff (A)

CB

when photocopying, align dotted rule with top edge of glass

agatha Ⓐ Ⓑ Ⓒ

enlarge all pattern pieces by 200%

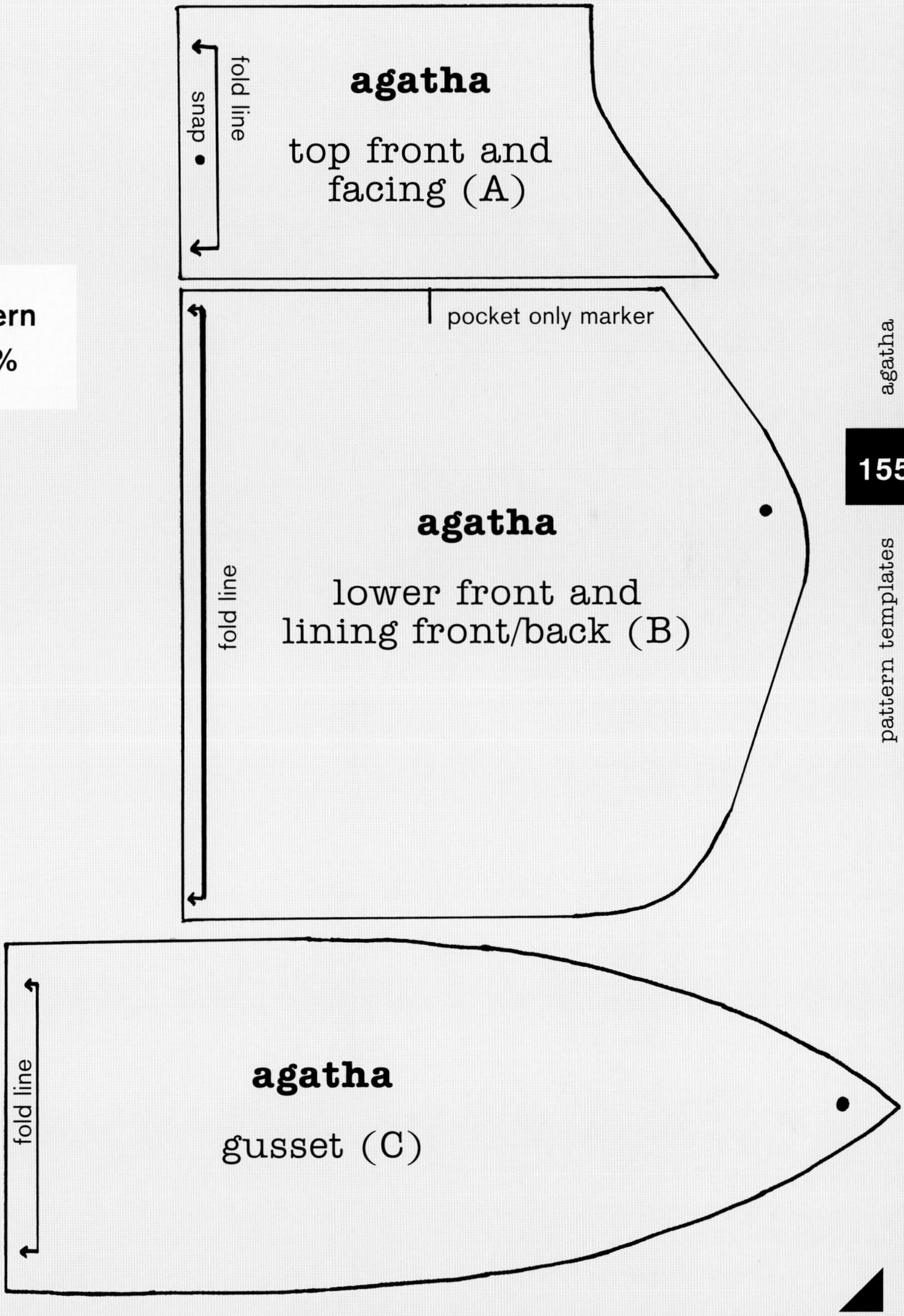

fold line

snap

snap •

agatha
top front and facing (A)

pocket only marker

fold line

agatha
lower front and lining front/back (B)

•

fold line

agatha
gusset (C)

•

ⓓ agatha

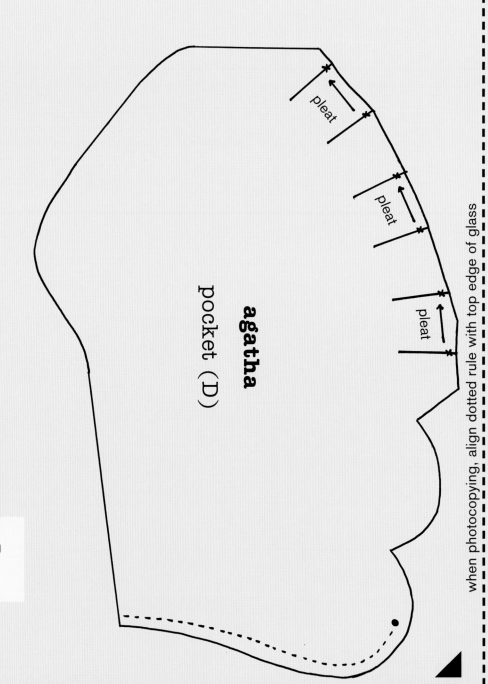

agatha
pocket (D)

pleat

pleat

pleat

when photocopying, align dotted rule with top edge of glass

**enlarge all pattern
pieces by 200%**

agatha

enlarge all pattern
pieces by 200%

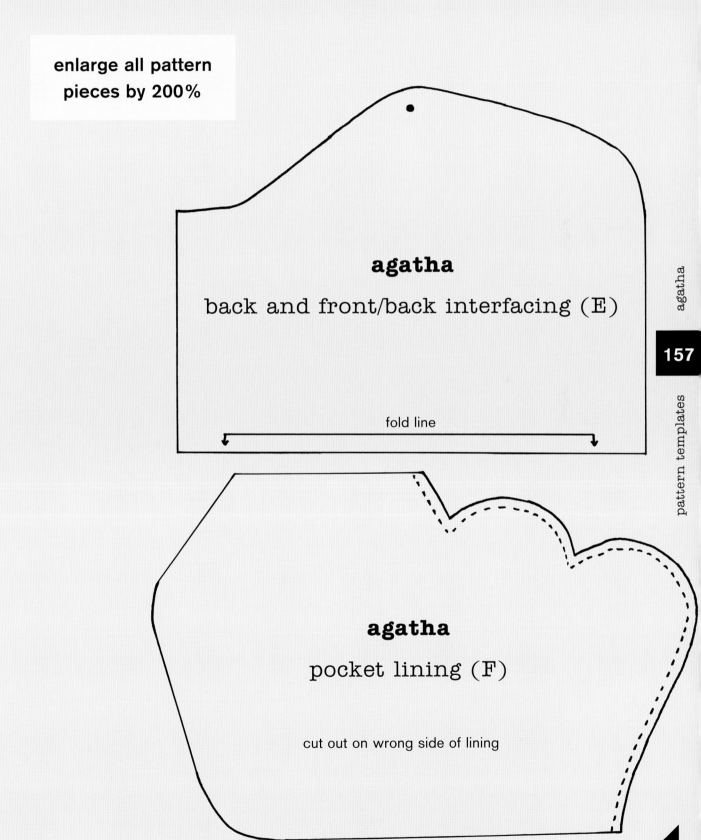

agatha

back and front/back interfacing (E)

fold line

agatha

pocket lining (F)

cut out on wrong side of lining

A **B** **lauren**

enlarge all pattern
pieces by 200%

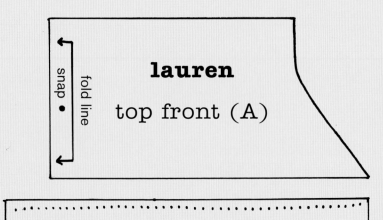

lauren

top front (A)

fold line

snap •

lauren

lower front side (B)

when photocopying, align dotted rule with top edge of glass

lauren

**enlarge all pattern
pieces by 200%**

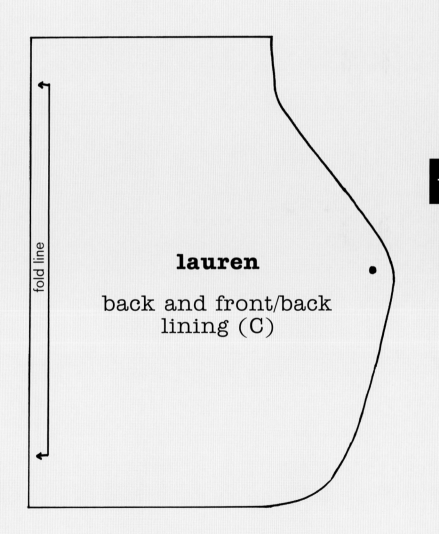

lauren

back and front/back
lining (C)

fold line

D E lauren

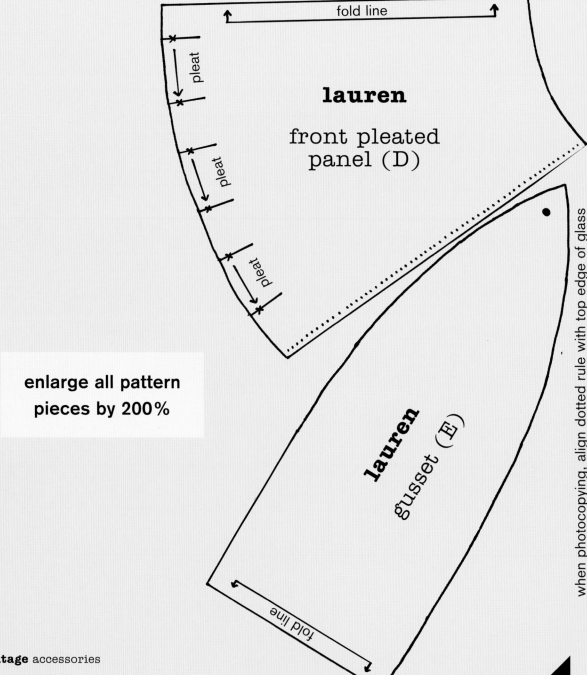

lauren
front pleated panel (D)

fold line

pleat

pleat

pleat

lauren
gusset (E)

fold line

when photocopying, align dotted rule with top edge of glass

enlarge all pattern pieces by 200%

lauren Ⓕ Ⓖ

enlarge all pattern
pieces by 200%

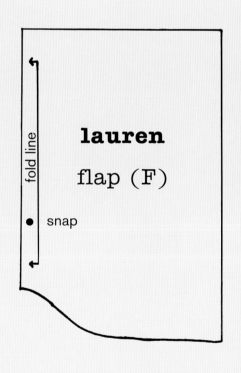

lauren

flap (F)

fold line

● snap

lauren

handle (G)

fold line

**enlarge all pattern
pieces by 200%**

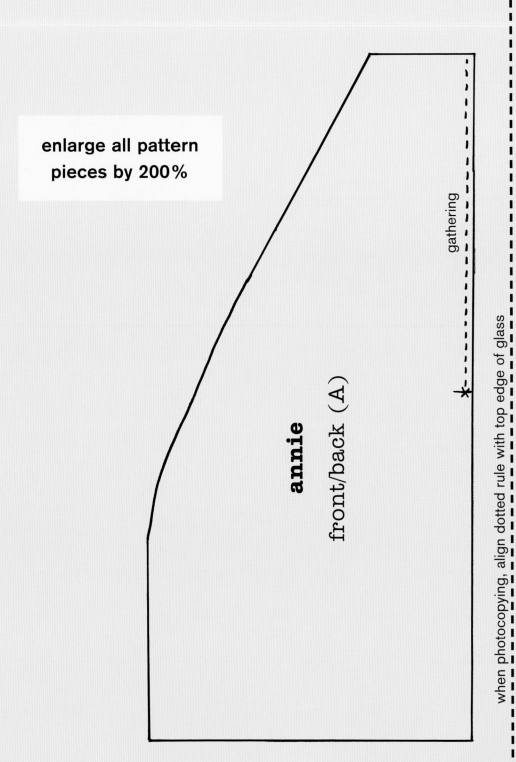

annie
front/back (A)

gathering

when photocopying, align dotted rule with top edge of glass

annie Ⓑ

enlarge all pattern
pieces by 200%

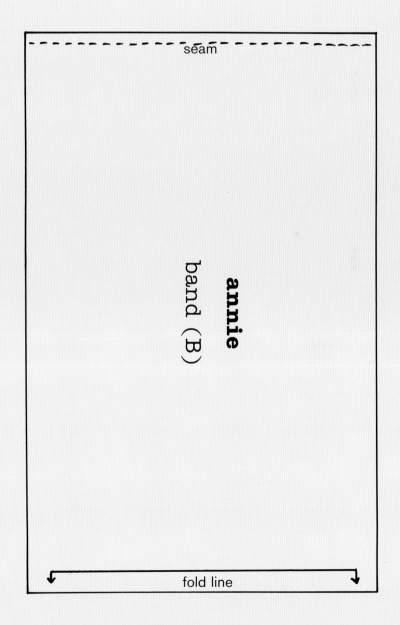

seam

annie
band (B)

fold line

enlarge all pattern pieces by 200%

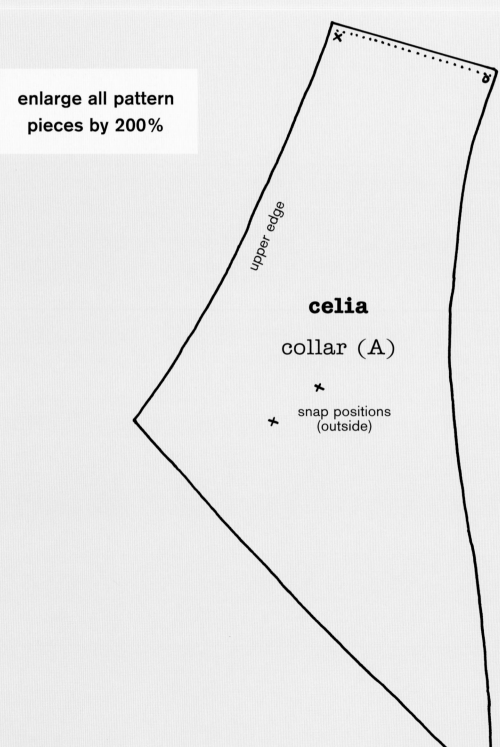

upper edge

celia

collar (A)

snap positions
(outside)

when photocopying, align dotted rule with top edge of glass

celia Ⓑ

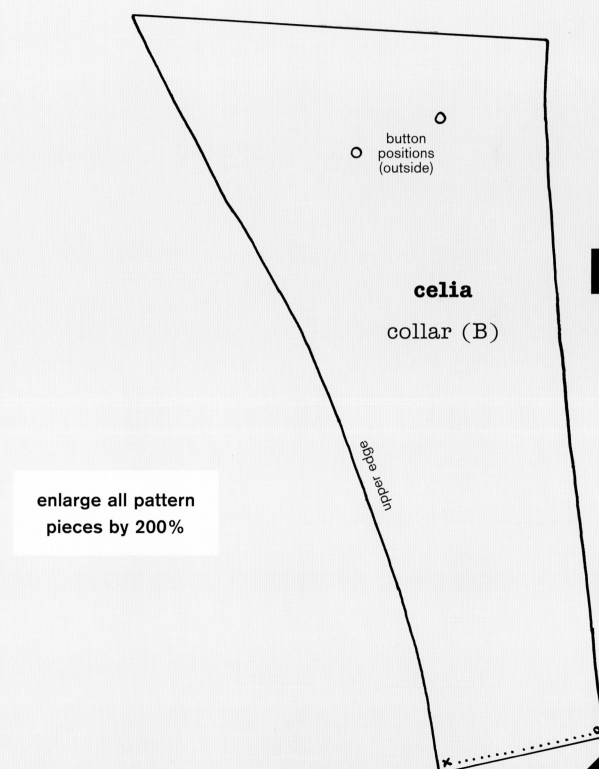

button
positions
(outside)

celia

collar (B)

upper edge

enlarge all pattern
pieces by 200%

166

enlarge all pattern
pieces by 200%

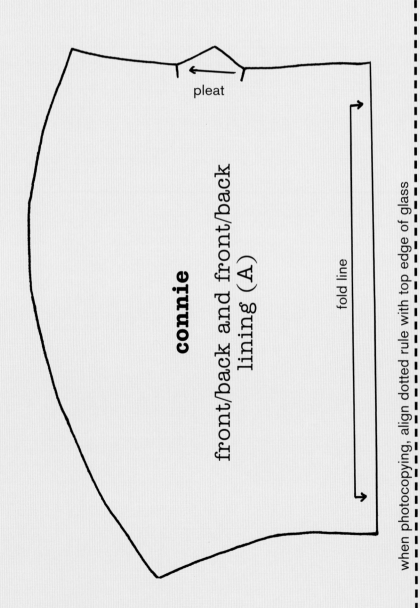

pleat

connie
front/back and front/back
lining (A)

fold line

when photocopying, align dotted rule with top edge of glass

connie **B C**

enlarge all pattern
pieces by 200%

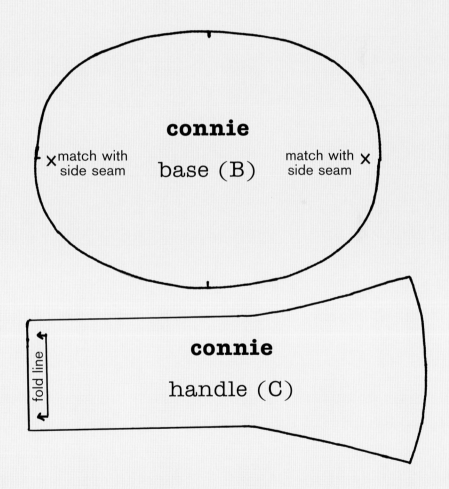

connie

base (B)

×match with
side seam

match with ×
side seam

connie

handle (C)

fold line

A B iris

enlarge all pattern
pieces by 200%

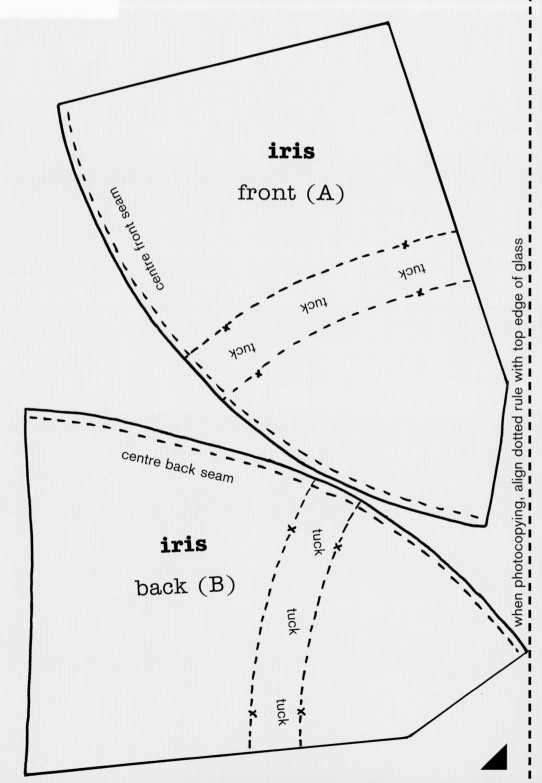

iris

front (A)

centre front seam

tuck

tuck

tuck

centre back seam

iris

back (B)

tuck

tuck

tuck

when photocopying, align dotted rule with top edge of glass

iris ©

enlarge all pattern
pieces by 200%

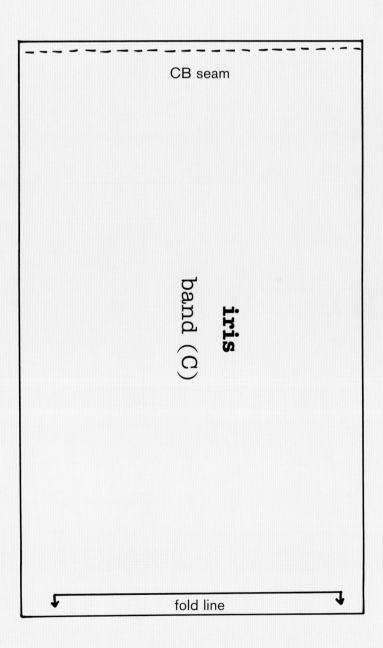

CB seam

iris
band (C)

fold line

enlarge all pattern pieces by 200%

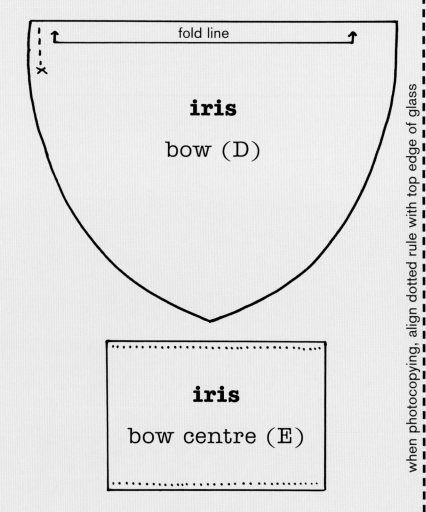

fold line

iris

bow (D)

iris

bow centre (E)

when photocopying, align dotted rule with top edge of glass

molly (A)

enlarge all pattern
pieces by 200%

fold line

molly

collar front/back (A)

making **vintage** accessories

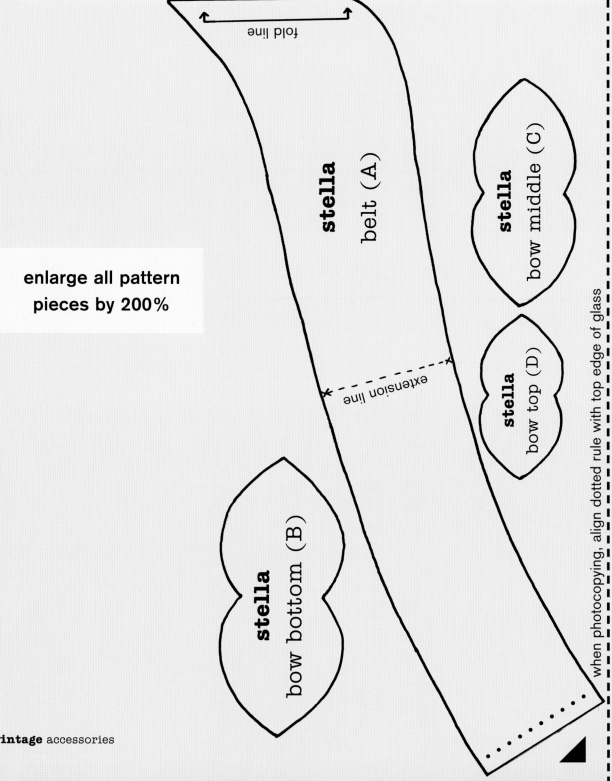

ABCD **stella**

enlarge all pattern
pieces by 200%

fold line

stella belt (A)

extension line

stella bow middle (C)

stella bow top (D)

stella bow bottom (B)

when photocopying, align dotted rule with top edge of glass

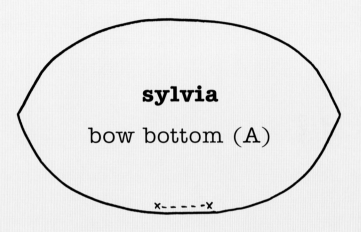

sylvia

bow bottom (A)

x------x

enlarge all pattern
pieces by 200%

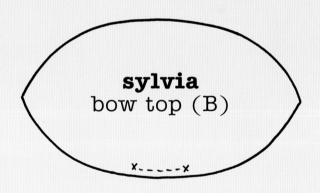

sylvia
bow top (B)

x------x

sylvia

bow centre tie (C)

x------x

enlarge all pattern
pieces by 200%

fold line

sylvia
cravat front/back (D)

when photocopying, align dotted rule with top edge of glass

cynthia  Ⓐ Ⓑ Ⓒ

enlarge all pattern
pieces by 200%

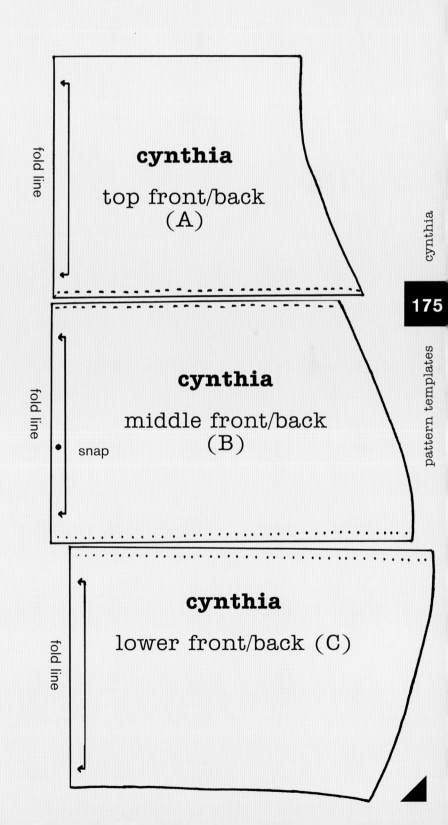

fold line

cynthia

top front/back
(A)

fold line

snap

cynthia

middle front/back
(B)

cynthia

lower front/back (C)

fold line

Ⓓ cynthia

enlarge all pattern pieces by 200%

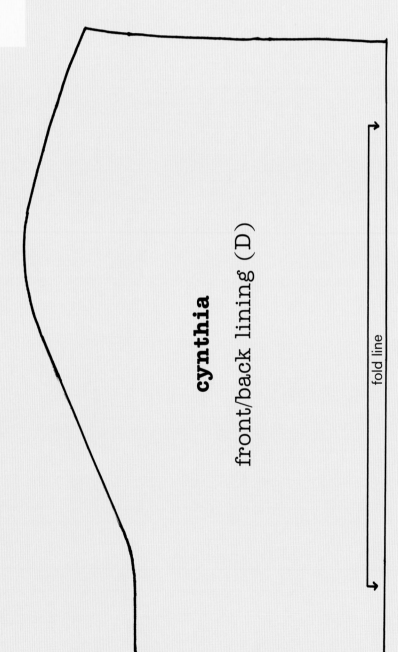

cynthia
front/back lining (D)

fold line

when photocopying, align dotted rule with top edge of glass

pattern templates

cynthia Ⓔ Ⓕ

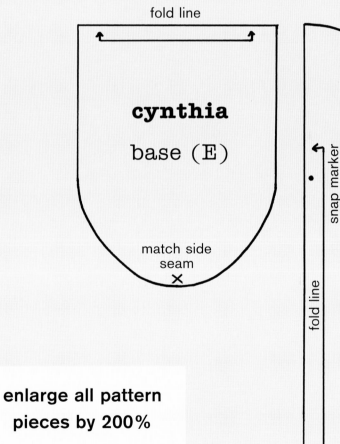

fold line

cynthia

base (E)

match side
seam
✕

fold line

snap marker

cynthia

flap (F)

enlarge all pattern
pieces by 200%

ⓖ **cynthia**

**enlarge all pattern
pieces by 200%**

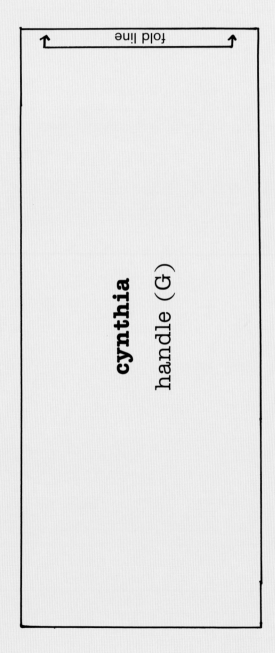

fold line

cynthia
handle (G)

when photocopying, align dotted rule with top edge of glass

sophia Ⓐ

enlarge all pattern
pieces by 200%

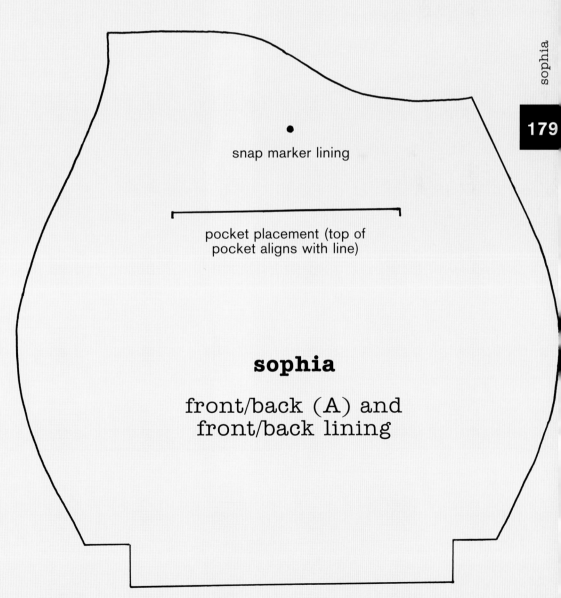

snap marker lining

pocket placement (top of
pocket aligns with line)

sophia

front/back (A) and
front/back lining

B C D E sophia

enlarge all pattern
pieces by 200%

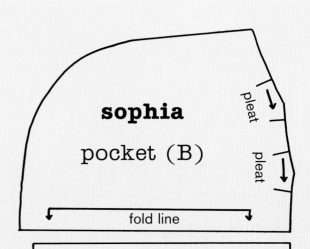

sophia

pocket (B)

pleat

pleat

fold line

sophia

pocket band (C)

sophia

pocket lining
(D)

fold line

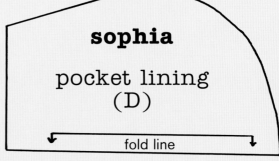

sophia

handle (E)

fold line

when photocopying, align dotted rule with top edge of glass

sophia **F**

enlarge all pattern
pieces by 200%

---

sophia

handle
tab (F)

---

daphne **A**

enlarge all pattern
pieces by 200%

fold line

daphne
side/back (A)

enlarge all pattern
pieces by 200%

fold line

daphne
top/front (B)

x

daphne
peak (C)

fold line

when photocopying, align dotted rule with top edge of glass

daphne

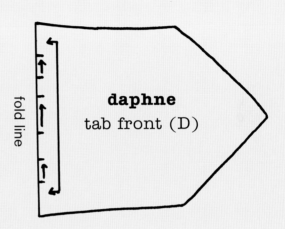

daphne
tab front (D)

fold line

enlarge all pattern
pieces by 200%

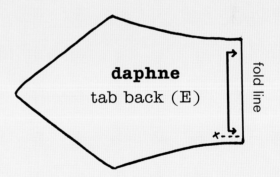

daphne
tab back (E)

fold line

daphne
tab centre (F)

Ⓐ jean

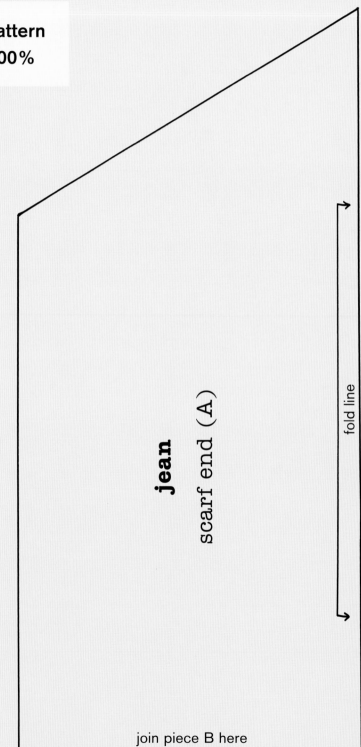

enlarge all pattern
pieces by 200%

jean
scarf end (A)

fold line

join piece B here

×

o

when photocopying, align dotted rule with top edge of glass

jean B C

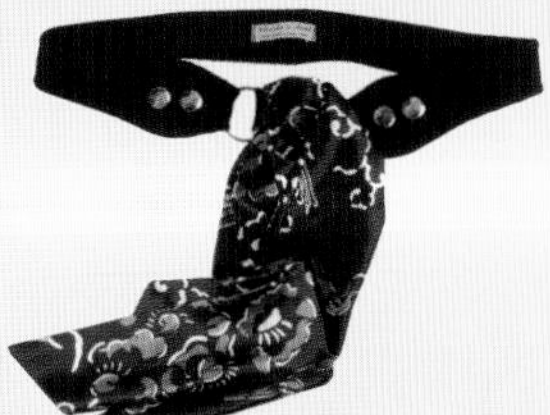

enlarge all pattern
pieces by 200%

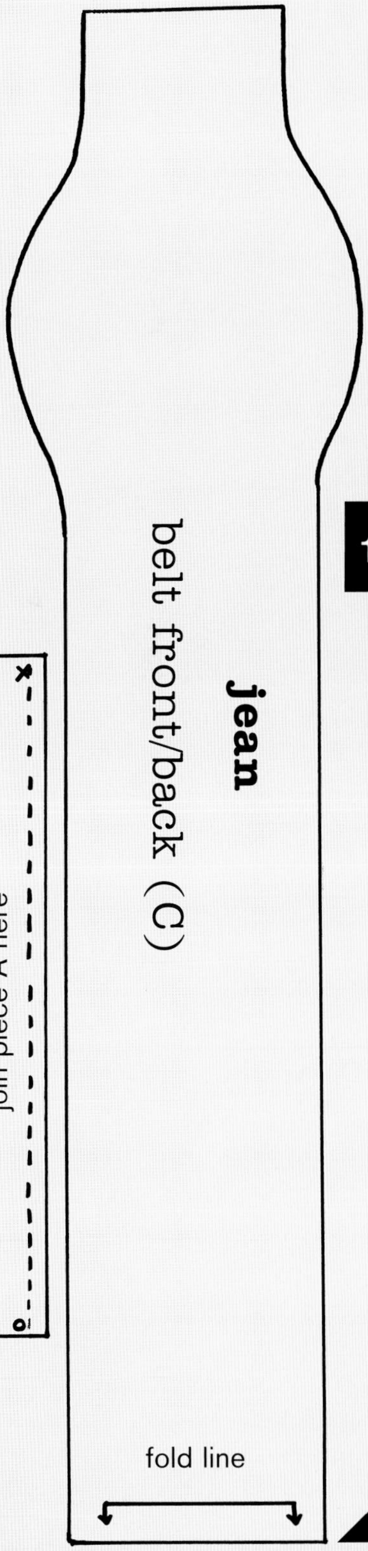

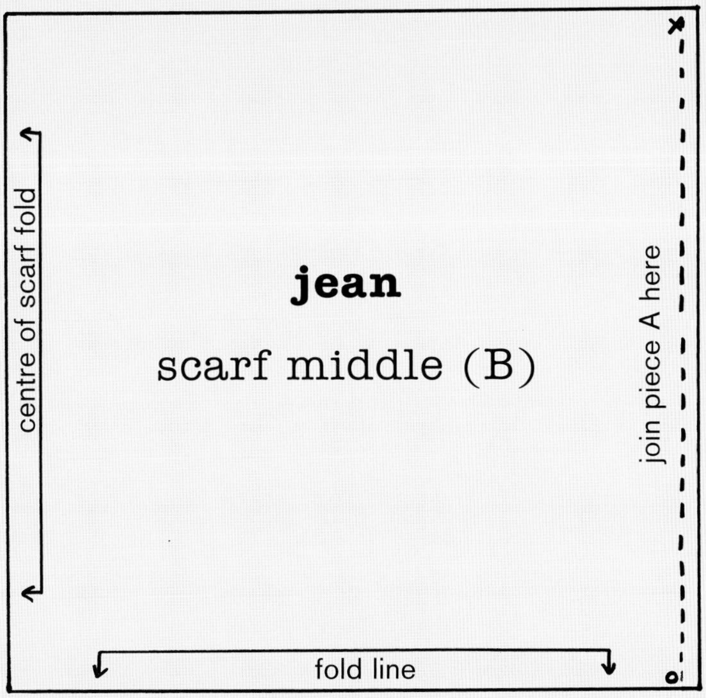

jean

belt front/back (C)

jean

scarf middle (B)

centre of scarf fold

join piece A here

fold line

fold line

Suppliers

Emma Brennan
For more information about Emma Brennan and her accessory designs, sewing patterns and kits, visit www.charliesaunt.com.

United Kingdom

Abakhan Fabrics
www.abakhan.co.uk
Online shop selling reasonably priced fabrics, including wool tweed, fake fur, fleece and velvet. The company also has seven retail outlets in the northwest of England.

FabricUK.com
Carlton Business Centre
132 Saltley Road
Birmingham
B7 4TH
Tel: 0870 170 1107
www.fabricuk.com
Online suppliers of a big ongoing range of fabrics including polyester/cotton quilted fabric ideal for use as a base/interfacing for bags and hats. Also stocks hard-wearing Melton wool fabric suitable for bags, and a selection of polar fleece.

Linton Tweeds Ltd
Shaddon Mills
Shaddongate
Carlisle
Cumbria CA2 5TZ
Tel: 01228 527569
www.lintondirect.com
Weavers and suppliers of wonderful designer 'Chanel' style tweeds.

MacCulloch & Wallis
25–26 Dering Street
London W1S 1AT
Tel: 0207 6290311
www.macculloch-wallis.co.uk
Suppliers of fabrics (from boiled wool to William Morris print quilting cottons), a small selection of bag handles and oodles of haberdashery items through mail order catalogue, online and shop.

Melin Tregwynt Millshop
Castlemorris
Haverfordwest
Pembrokeshire
SA62 5UX
Mail order tel: 01348 891644
www.melintregwynt.co.uk
Weavers of outstanding traditional wool fabrics with a contemporary edge in signature patterns such as the 'Mondo' spotted tweed used in Connie, on pages 98–9.

Planet Fleece Ltd
21a Whitehorse St
Baldock
Herts
SG7 6QB
Tel: 01462 491500
www.planetfleece.co.uk
Online suppliers of very good quality polar fleece fabrics for hats and scarves.

Rapture & Wright
www.raptureandwright.co.uk
Tel: 01608 652442
Hand-printed designer decorator fabrics suitable for making bags

United States

www.embellishedseams.com
Online suppliers of lace motifs and appliqués suitable for dyeing and hand painting, alongside a small selection of beads and trims.

www.emmaonesock.com
Online supplier of stunning designer fabrics including Italian wool coatings. The site is updated regularly and stocks small quantities of exclusive designs, ideal for fashion accessories.

www.gemsandknots.com
Online supplier of vintage Lucite beads and pendants for adding genuine vintage elements to your handmade rickrack jewellery and button badges.

Australia

Mill Direct Textiles LLC
15 Union Street
Lawrence
MA 01840
www.milldirecttextiles.com
Suppliers of polar fleece fabrics.

www.sovintagepatterns.com
*Online suppliers of original vintage
sewing patterns, including bags
and hats.*

The Beadin' Path, Inc
15 Main Street
Freeport
Maine 04032
www.beadinpath.com
*Online suppliers of new and
vintage glass beads, vintage
Lucite beads, vintage pendants
and unusual metal beads and
components.*

www.vintagefashionlibrary.com
*Original and reproduction sewing
patterns from 1850s to 1970s*

Vintage Vogue
712 June Drive
Corona
California,
92879 – 1143
USA
www.vintagevogue.com
*Online suppliers of ribbons, wool
felt, purse patterns and books.*

www.funkyfabrixonline.com
*Online suppliers of 'retro modern'
fabrics including hand-printed
cottons, Japanese fabrics and
home decor fabrics suitable for
making fashion accessories.*

Ozbeads
12 Curzon Street
Toowoomba
Queensland 4350
www.ozbeads.com.au
*Suppliers of beads including
Indian glass mixes, freshwater
pearls, antique finish metal and
semi-precious beads.*

**Sanshi (Fabrics and Fibres
from Japan)**
119 Solomon Street
Beaconsfield
Western Australia 6162
www.sanshi.com.au
*This online company offers
beautiful Japanese fabrics in
a wide range of cotton prints,
kimono fabrics and vintage textiles.
Ideal for piecing if you want
something different from the usual
quilting prints.*

Specklefarm
(Store) 111, Bridport Street
Albert Park
Victoria 3207
www.specklefarm.com.au
*Range of adorable own-design
striped and stitched grosgrain
ribbons and ribbon-covered
buttons.*

**Tall Poppy Craft Products Pty
Limited**
P O Box 391
Hurstville BC NSW 1481
Sydney
Tel: 02 8003 7140
www.tallpoppycraft.com
(Also have a sub-branch in the US)
*Suppliers of handbag handles,
snaps and other related products
for making accessories*

Also in Australia, the national chain
of Spotlight stores stocks a huge
range of fabric and craft items.
Spotlight has rickrack trims in a
range of colours and widths, and
usually carries a good stock of
polar fleece in varying weights,
wool fabrics in the winter and
the quilted calico fabric used as
interfacing throughout this book.

acknowledgements

GMC Publications would like to thank the following for their help with this book:

The Boxroom, The Old Needlemakers, West Street, Lewes, BN7 2NZ.Tel: 01273 476001.
Vintage Costume and Accessories.

Virginia Brehaut, Emma Foster, Anna de Lanoy, Rebecca Mothersole, Gilda Pacitti, Gill Parris, and Georgina Taylor, for lending props and accessories.

The author would like to thank the following people for their help in producing this book:

Will Russell for his technical expertise, and oodles of patience taking the step-by-step photographs (especially when I spilled hot tea over his dining room table in the lace-dyeing stage!).

Thanks to Carmen Allan for providing the hands for the how-to photographs over a gruelling five hours with very little complaint.

Also thanks to Gerrie Purcell for believing in my work, to Gilda Pacitti for her artistic knowledge and to Virginia Brehaut for meticulous editing.

Thanks to my dear friends Andy, Lindsay, Kate and Dan in Australia for keeping me sane during a very difficult period. Eternal gratitude and love to my wonderful mother and nephew Charlie in the UK for always being there for me no matter what. Thanks also to Shirley for never forgetting me.

The great memories of my dear father and sister continue to be my biggest source of inspiration.

index

Page numbers in **bold** refer to illustrations

To place an order, or to request a catalogue, contact:

GMC Publications Ltd

Castle Place, 166 High Street, Lewes, East Sussex, BN7 1XU

United Kingdom

Tel: 01273 488005   **Fax:** 01273 402866

Website: www.gmcbooks.com

Orders by credit card are accepted